A STORY OF KARMA

A
STORY OF
KARMA

FINDING LOVE AND TRUTH
IN THE LOST VALLEY
OF THE HIMALAYA

MICHAEL SCHAUCH

RMB

For information on purchasing bulk quantities of this book, or to
obtain media excerpts or invite the author to speak at an event,
please visit rmbooks.com and select the "Contact" tab.

RMB | Rocky Mountain Books Ltd.
rmbooks.com
@rmbooks
facebook.com/rmbooks

Cataloguing data available from Library and Archives Canada
ISBN 9781771604673 (paperback)
ISBN 9781771604680 (electronic)

All photographs are by the author unless otherwise noted.

Design: Chyla Cardinal

Printed and bound in Canada

We would like to also take this opportunity to acknowledge the traditional
territories upon which we live and work. In Calgary, Alberta, we acknowledge
the Niitsítapi (Blackfoot) and the people of the Treaty 7 region in Southern
Alberta, which includes the Siksika, the Piikuni, the Kainai, the Tsuut'ina and
the Stoney Nakoda First Nations, including Chiniki, Bearpaw, and Wesley First
Nations. The City of Calgary is also home to Métis Nation of Alberta, Region
III. In Victoria, British Columbia, we acknowledge the traditional territories
of the Lkwungen (Esquimalt, and Songhees), Malahat, Pacheedaht, Scia'new,
T'Sou-ke and W̱SÁNEĆ (Pauquachin, Tsartlip, Tsawout, Tseycum) peoples.

We acknowledge the financial support of the Government of Canada
through the Canada Book Fund and the Canada Council for the
Arts, and of the province of British Columbia through the British
Columbia Arts Council and the Book Publishing Tax Credit.

Disclaimer
The views expressed in this book are those of the author and do not
necessarily reflect those of the publishing company, its staff or its affiliates.

For Mom and Dad.

The softest things in the world
overcome the hardest things in the world.

—LAO TZU, *TAO TE CHING*

CONTENTS

PRELUDE

Outside the snow crystals danced in spirals, as if stirred by an invisible angry force. Some eventually came to rest on the ground, blanketing the landscape. Others returned to the sky, becoming lost in the infinite white that had now become our world.

My two Nepali guides and I had taken refuge in the ruins of an ancient stone hut. It was one of a number of huts – in varying degrees of collapse – that must have once been part of a great village, though all other signs of human habitation had disappeared. We sat in silence on the frozen dirt with our backs to the wall, looking out through what would have been a doorway but was now just an empty space, listening to the mountain winds exhale. Towers of ice and rock as high as 7000 metres surrounded us like a fortress. They held the authority out here. The three of us, IC, Ngawang and I, were deep in the remote Himalaya of northern Nepal, isolated not just from the rest of the world but also from our companions – my wife, our three friends and the other members of our team – who had remained behind. They were in a village not far away, but at the moment they might as well have been on the other side of the world, our aloneness seemed so complete.

Some might have wondered why I had gone through so much effort, time and money to venture into this desert of ice and rock in one of the most far-flung, inhospitable and even dangerous places on Earth. I know my parents had asked me the question enough times. I could never really give them a reason. The mountains called to me, and I went to them. I'd been answering that call in many places over many years, though never in a place as remote as this.

My wife, Chantal, who was further down the valley, waiting for us to return, had tried her best to support me on this expedition, as she had on so many others. She understood how important it was to me, and she had wanted me to climb my mountain. But I never imagined this journey would take such a severe toll on her. Although she had gone on a number of these expeditions with me, including a recent one that she herself had suggested to Mount Kilimanjaro, trekking through these mountains in the thin, high-altitude air had been much harder for her, both physically and mentally, than either of us had anticipated. It was my ambition that had brought us here, and now it had taken me away from her, away from what mattered most. A shiver ran up my spine. I pulled the collar of my jacket over my mouth and breathed into it, feeling the warmth for a moment against my neck.

"What is this place?" I wondered aloud, speaking to no one in particular.

Ngawang's eyes narrowed, studying the wall in front of us, as though each of its stones had a story trapped inside. "This place is empty. Villagers left long time."

Our hut was no more than four walls of rock stacked about two metres high, bound together by caked mud, with a roof also made of stones, which was supported by wooden beams. The stones were rough and cold to the touch. The whole place smelled of ice and earth. It smelled old. A single ray of light reflecting off the snow outside lit the dim room through the opening at the front.

My eyes traced a crack in the rock wall that ran from the dirt floor up to the beams above me. The beams were also fractured, some of them nearly split in two and caving in from the weight of the large flat stones of the roof. The whole thing looked like it was destined to collapse on us at any moment. But it wasn't the thought of being buried by the rocks that bothered me most – it was the possibility that no one would ever find us here, amid the many other piles of rocks in what was left of this Himalayan ghost town.

The remnants of the village appeared to be centuries old. The rocks of which the houses had been constructed were reduced to rubble, weathered and faded, covered in red lichen and inscribed with Tibetan etchings unlike any we had seen before, as though from another era. These few human-made markings would soon become invisible, time and weather erasing all traces of the people who had lived here under what must have been extreme hardship.

The only sign of life we had encountered nearby was the print left by a snow leopard. We had discovered it just before getting trapped by the storm. I took comfort in thinking about the snow leopard – a creature that had somehow managed to live within this barren, isolated place. I had imagined it watching us as we fumbled our way forward through the blizzard. How very different it was from me – a living being as fluid as a mountain stream, and as ghostly as the summit we sought to climb. Yet for all our differences, I felt a kinship with it, a sense that both of us had been called to the mountain that loomed above us, that this was where we were both meant to be.

And it wasn't just any mountain. It was *the* mountain. A perfect pyramid from its southwest aspect, with sheer faces and a striking ridgeline that snaked its way to a spear-tipped summit piercing both cloud and sky. It was a mountain out of a storybook. I yearned to feel it beneath my feet. To climb it, to experience it, to learn from it, to be part of it – even if only for a brief moment. It had won my heart and beckoned me to come to it. It was a jewel of the earth, buried deep in the Himalaya. And I had found it.

From the moment I first saw it – in a photo a friend had shown me in a restaurant some months before – I couldn't stop thinking about it. It was a place I seemed to have imagined in my dreams; one I felt I had to find in real life. The pyramid mountain drove me into a fit of mountain frenzy – one that consumed me, forcing me on a mad quest into one of the most inaccessible corners of Nepal, where we had come up against a wall of mountains called the Lugula in the upper Manang district, a distant sub-range of the Himalaya that formed part of the border between Nepal and Tibet. Thrust up from the Tibetan plateau, the chain of 6000–7000-metre jaw-dropping peaks formed a serrated horizon so high that even the clouds gazed up to it.

Yet for all the awe I felt in the presence of these Himalayan peaks, there was something equally powerful about the valley where our companions were now sheltering. I had felt something there I had never experienced before – a sense that I had travelled into another world, but also that it was a world I'd been to before. It was as though I was a time traveller from the future who had stumbled my way back into a different epoch, one I had somehow known in an age long forgotten and was meant to return to.

The few mountain dwellers we had come in contact with over the previous days had reinforced these strange sensations. I'd seen them only briefly as we passed each other on the mountain paths. But I'd felt drawn to them, as if they possessed some deep wisdom I'd lost but could learn again if only there were time. Yet we had forged past them, driven by my compulsion to keep moving, venturing ever deeper into the mountains, until they became mere dots of colour against the barren landscape, and then disappeared entirely.

They left my sight, but they did not leave my heart. Who were these Himalayan wanderers? What pulled me to them? I had so many questions. Questions that seemed destined to go unanswered, for my focus on the pyramid mountain was absolute, and I was determined that nothing would get in the way of my ambition to scale it.

We'd been trekking for nearly two weeks by then with our companions, and then venturing out on our own, on this mission to find the pyramid mountain, for the last two days. During these two days alone, my Nepali guides and I had crossed many distant rivers and explored outlying valleys and ridges, had covered 30 kilometres and ascended nearly 1850 metres. I had spent over 15 years training in the mountains to be in a place like this, to climb that mountain that lay so tantalizingly before us – only to find myself caught in a snowstorm.

As I contemplated our next step, the snow crystals outside began floating their way across the exposed threshold, turning to frost on my face and numbing it. Even with my merino wool base layer, microfibre fleece, 800 fill goose down jacket and windbreaker, I was cold. My body was starting to feel fatigued, partly from the chill that was sapping the energy out of me, and partly from the 5030-metre elevation, which was making me feel short of breath.

The longer we stayed here the worse it was going to get. We had to leave. I peered outside. Our plan to wait out the storm had failed; it was clear the snowstorm wasn't going to let up.

I looked over at IC and Ngawang. Their faces, once ablaze with mountain fever, were now weary, anxious. We didn't speak, but we knew what we had to do. Lifting ourselves from the frozen earth, we brushed off the frost and shouldered our backpacks. We fastened our jackets and cinched our hoods around our faces. And then, one by one, we ducked through the doorway and into the whirling whiteness. With luck we could make our way back to the village before night fell. I felt defeated, but I also felt we had no choice but to return.

PART ONE

THE PYRAMID MOUNTAIN

ONE

Chantal and I were coming to the end of a long evening we had shared with a new and fascinating acquaintance, an evening that had already resulted in a plan for a journey to a land thousands of kilometres away. But then something drew my attention.

"What is this mountain?" I asked, looking at one of Mick's photos he had just pulled up on his phone. The mountain was shaped like a perfect pyramid, as if some divine force had sculpted it with a knife, crowning it with an ice- and snow-clad peak that reached high above the clouds.

"I have no idea. I don't know if it even has a name," Mick replied.

The thought of a mountain that wasn't just awe-inspiring but a mystery made it all the more alluring. I couldn't take my eyes off the photo. I was mesmerized by it. And for a moment there was a lull in the high-energy wall of sound in Vancouver's chic Yaletown restaurant. Electronic beats hushed. Chatter quieted. Neon lights softened. It was as though the entire restaurant felt the same sense of awe I was feeling. As the three of us sat there in our own bubble, oblivious to the Friday night crowd around us, Mick and Chantal watched me, aware that something had struck a profound chord in me.

Chantal and I had met Mick at exactly the right time. It was 2011. We had just come off leading two major mountain-climbing expeditions, one in Mexico a few months before, and one in Africa in 2010, and we were eager to embark on our next adventure, whatever it might be. So it was serendipitous that Mick entered our lives just then. He was a free-spirited Brit who had escaped the UK for the remote hippy island life of the rugged Canadian west coast. He was unconventional, loved the outdoors and had a particular passion for trekking in the Himalaya. In fact, he had spent the last 20 years venturing into some of the most remote and lesser known areas of Nepal and had founded his own travel company, Wilderness Trekking, in 2006. He was the real deal.

Both Chantal and I had always been drawn to nature, though Chantal's interest in mountaineering was relatively recent, inspired by my own. We had met in university, and it wasn't long before we became sweethearts. When I first saw her, in the auditorium at the University of Victoria, where some 150 students who were entering the bachelor of commerce program were introducing themselves, one by one, in brief 30-second bios, I immediately knew she was special. And it wasn't because of her Swiss accent, or the European flair she exuded with her style and quiet confidence. No, there was an air of innocence and playfulness in her sky-blue eyes that enchanted me. But I could also sense strength of mind and steadfast determination that was not to be trifled with. The more I got to know her, the more my initial impressions would turn out to be true.

Prior to entering the world of business, Chantal had spent most of her youth training as a classical violinist. Years upon years of hard work afforded her a spot in the Eastman School of Music at the University of Rochester in New York, one of the top music schools in the world. But after a year at the school she was crushed by the realization that pursuing a life as a professional musician – a life of relentless psychological and physical pressure – had not only sucked the joy out of playing her instrument, it had also left her suffering from severe performance anxiety. She made the bold move to leave the school, and with it her desire to pursue music as a career. Since she had grown up with a father who was a successful entrepreneur, it was a natural decision for her to change her focus to the world of business.

When we met each other, at a time when she was just emerging from the stresses that had led her to rethink her career path, I think what struck her first about me was my spontaneity and love for life, which were so completely different from the often grim intensity of those in her former music circles. I had a laugh she could identify from half a mile away, and an optimism that was so unremitting that I think it sometimes got on her nerves. With my hands stained from chalk from my stints at the climbing gym between classes, and my baggy jeans and fitted T-shirts, I might not have seemed serious about my studies. But I was also the only one in our entire cohort who was running a successful business on the side – one I'd started in high school with an unrealistic dream but had since grown into a national distributor of designer kitchenware.

On top of this, I think she found my eclectic family background appealing, since it in some ways resembled her own. She had been born in Switzerland and lived there until she was 13, when her parents moved to Canada. My father had emigrated from Germany, my mother was born in Macau and had grown up in Hong Kong and I grew up in a sleepy farming community on the west coast of Canada (the kind of community where kids would ask why I was always tanned, and why my mom spoke "funny").

This eclecticism was reflected in my habits and interests. In my room, Chantal would find the Bach, Vivaldi, Mozart and Handel albums she was familiar with, but they were interspersed with Rage Against the Machine, Daft Punk, Jimi Hendrix and Our Lady Peace. On my bedside table, books by Goethe, Homer, Tolkien and Jon Krakauer alternated with climbing guides and volumes on Zen Buddhism. In my closet the neatly pressed dress shirts and suits I needed for business meetings hung alongside a rack of climbing gear.

Both our differences and our similarities were reflected in our feelings about the mountains. Growing up in Switzerland, surrounded by mountains and lakes, Chantal felt deeply connected to nature, and had loved taking long walks in the beautiful landscapes of her homeland. This connection was strengthened when her family moved to the west coast of Canada, but she had lost it during the years of her intense immersion in music. By the time I met her, she had a deep desire to rediscover the joy she had once found in nature, and this seemed like a natural fit with my own way of life.

We began spending a lot of time hiking together, which we both loved. But mountain climbing was a whole different thing. If anything, it seemed to drive us apart rather than bring us closer. While Chantal loved hearing about my adventures, she didn't think she had the strength or endurance to join me on them, and the amount of time I spent pursuing my mountaineering objectives left her feeling abandoned and alone.

When Chantal felt our relationship drifting, she approached the problem like the planner she was. One day in 2008, seven years into our relationship, she came to me with the idea of climbing Mount Kilimanjaro together. Goal-oriented and methodical, she gave herself two years to get into shape for it, working with a personal trainer to retrain both her muscles and her mind for the challenges ahead. She set "practice" mountain objectives for herself, and together we went on small scrambles on the west coast that turned into larger ones like Mount Temple in the Canadian Rockies, and even higher ones in Mexico and Switzerland. They didn't always have to be the hardest or the highest mountains. For her, the point was to enjoy the time she spent there, while getting ever stronger and fitter. For me, any chance to be on a mountain, especially with Chantal, was a good one.

Slowly but surely Chantal took to mountaineering, particularly to the flow and pacing that are typical of climbing volcanoes. She loved the long meditative slogs up the steep snow slopes of volcanoes like Mount Baker in Washington or Mount Hood in Oregon. There she could get into her own rhythm, challenging herself beyond what she thought possible, and tuning out the expectations of daily life. This became particularly important to her after she had worked herself into the marketing communications rat race, a world filled with tough deadlines and competition among consultants vying for new contracts. It was the mountains that offered her solace then – and because of her intensity, she needed that solace.

I had learned early in our relationship that whatever Chantal pursued, she put her whole heart into it. She owned it as though her life was on the line, sometimes to her own detriment because of the pressure she put on herself. I learned about the agonizing, self-doubting inner dialogues that played out in her mind. I learned about the chronic pain that would attack her body. Often it struck out of nowhere. I learned that, since she was a teenager, she had suffered from debilitating migraine attacks that would leave her lifeless and retching – sometimes for days at a time. The mountains became a way for her to look beyond all of that. They gave her the space to breathe, to reflect, to reconnect with herself. They were her place of escape and healing.

My relationship to the mountains had always been very different. I didn't want to escape intensity but to dive into it, and the mountains were my portal. My craving to climb them was so obsessive that it was like an addiction. I wanted not only to get to the summit but to experience my whole body straining to get there, to feel the rock and the ice on every step of the journey to the top. I loved the rawness and the beauty of the mountains, the way they heightened my sensitivity to everything. The mountains taught me some of my greatest life lessons. They pushed me to the brink of my abilities. They grounded me. They lifted me up. They kept me honest. Always changing, as the forces of nature and time reshaped them, sometimes over millennia, sometimes in the space of a day under the pressure of rockslides and earthquakes, they conditioned me to accept change too. They taught me about myself. They became a part of me. I often relied upon them for guidance, both in and out of the boardroom. Above all, I had a deep respect for them.

Over time, the mountains created a focal point for Chantal and me. They gave us a place to find deeper meaning not only within ourselves but also in each other. Somehow, through our shared love of the mountains, all the apparent discordances between us added up to harmony. Together, we found a new rhythm.

As Chantal grew stronger and we began making our plans to climb Mount Kilimanjaro – the mountain she'd been training for over the last two years – I was thrilled we would be taking on this challenge together. This would be a real triumph for her. But she decided she wanted to do it for a cause bigger than herself. Because of her gratitude for the relief her time in the mountains had given her from the migraines that had plagued her ever since childhood, she wanted to use the climb to raise funds for a local charity that helped youths living with mental and physical disabilities to gain access to nature. I was fully on board. After all, the mountains and nature had made me who I am. I couldn't imagine what would have become of me had I not had those opportunities. Yet for all the years I had been climbing, I had always climbed for my own satisfaction. It was Chantal who taught me to think how I could bring that joy to others.

After enlisting fundraisers who agreed to donate to the charity we'd chosen, we led a team of 12 to the summit of Mount Kilimanjaro to Uhuru Peak ("uhuru" being the Swahili word for "freedom"). Off the back of that, we led another team on a fundraising expedition down to Mexico where we climbed Mexican volcanoes, including Pico de Orizaba, the third-highest peak in North America. Within 13 months, our teams had raised over $200,000 for the charity. And we became hooked. Hooked not just on the mountaineering, but on venturing out for something greater than ourselves. And that was when my sights turned to Nepal. Or should I say returned to Nepal.

I believe that for each of us there is a place that pulls at the very core of our souls. Some of us eventually find our way there. Others don't. For me, Nepal was that place. For as long as I could remember, and even though I had never set foot there, I had always felt a deep connection to Nepal. I yearned to experience its culture, its magnificent sights, its people. When I was 17 years old, my sister gave me a Lonely Planet book called *Trekking in the Nepal Himalaya* for Christmas. It was the best present I'd ever received. I'll never forget the morning I unwrapped that book. Gripped immediately by its cover, I couldn't stop looking at it. In the background was an image of the mighty Kanchenjunga, the third-highest mountain in the world, and in the foreground was a string of colourful prayer flags, pointing to the mountain's snow-crested summit. I obsessively pored over the book, flipping from one page to the next so fast I couldn't even read the text. One moment I was gawking at images of soaring mountains and endless glaciers; the next I was absorbed by portraits of bronze-faced Nepalis adorned in strange headdresses, colourful robes, golden nose rings and hooped earrings. The old looked as joyful and light-hearted as the young.

There were weathered mani walls, some as tall as four metres or more, constructed of rocks etched with strange inscriptions. There were also long rows of chortens, the iconic Buddhist stone structures that are seen throughout the Himalaya, often at the entrances to villages or in mountain passes or at bridges – places that are seen as thresholds in need of the protection offered by the prayers and relics placed within the chortens. There were maps dotted out with trekking routes and exotic-sounding village names, alongside images of mountain villages that looked right out of a *National Geographic* magazine. There were pictures of traditional Nepali festivals – people dressed in vibrant ethnic costumes and masks, everyone arrayed in what appeared to be an elaborate dance. It was all too much. I was overdosing on exhilaration. All I wanted to do was to blast out of the house in my robe and slippers, Lonely Planet book in hand, and fly over to Nepal at once.

And then things happened. "Life," as it were, got in the way. During a very busy 15 years, I went to university while continuing to run the kitchenware business I had started in high school, became interested in investing, went to graduate school and got my master's degree in business, launched a career focused on investing and financial services and eventually started a practice with my business partner to provide wealth management expertise for a group of several dozen high net worth families. Before long, years had passed and I was in my early 30s. At first, school and a lack of funds had held me back. Later on, with my career and business, I had the money but not the time.

Besides, I could never quite settle on what I actually wanted to *do* in Nepal. Did I want to climb a mountain? Which one? Did I want to do a long backpacking trip? Would it be Everest base camp? Annapurna Circuit? Nothing really seemed to stick. I know it would have seemed like a good idea to just go and have an experience. But Nepal to me was this mystical place, a place out of my wildest fantasies, and if I were to go I wanted to do something truly unique, something to do justice to its specialness. I wanted to go somewhere off the beaten path, deep in the mountains where no one else was going, in search for something – in search for myself. I was desperately romantic about it all, but that's what I was set on. The more I racked my brain over what the perfect trip would be, however, the more other adventures found their way into my life, pushing Nepal further away and landing it on a perpetual backburner.

That is, until the night Chantal and I found ourselves in the middle of a chic Vancouver restaurant, sitting across from that rugged, poncho-wearing, British-accented west coast islander. Talking to Mick felt like being with an old friend. We understood each other instinctively. And his profound love for Nepal, which was reflected in the gentleness that came over his expression when he spoke of that faraway place and its people, rekindled the old flame in my own heart. He could see it in my eyes – just as I could see it in his.

"Let me tell you about the Lost Valley of Nar Phu," Mick had said at the beginning of the evening. He had me at "lost valley." At the time, it was an all but unknown valley in one of the most isolated, far northern corners of the Nepal Himalaya bordering Tibet. Until recently, it had been totally closed off to outsiders. A remote hidden valley, an ancient mountain culture, unknown peaks: everything he said about it was perfect. Mick regaled us with stories from his journeys into the area as we scanned through his pictures. The images of the villages blew my mind. I felt like I was looking at fairy tale mountain kingdoms from "once upon a time." Except they were real, and they were now. But how long could that fairy tale last? Because mountaineers and trekkers had begun to make their way into these remote places, it seemed possible they wouldn't stay that way for much longer.

The photos of the people particularly captivated me. They looked like the people I had seen nearly 15 years before in the Lonely Planet book my sister had given me. Mick had a tremendous love for the villagers of the Lost Valley. And he was concerned about them too. About the fact that their culture would experience unprecedented pressure to change now that the valley had been opened to the outside world. About how – or whether – they would be able to adapt. About whether the forces of modernity would alter them irrevocably, causing them to lose touch with their culture and its traditions. As he spoke, I imagined these villagers exposed to our modern world, to the forces of globalization and assimilation, consumerism and popular culture that had permeated – and dominated – seemingly every corner of the globe in recent decades.

And yet, relative to the way of life of the nomadic villagers I saw in Mick's pictures, which had existed for centuries, perhaps millennia, our own way of life had existed for only the blink of an eye. Isolated from the rest of the world, the mountain dwellers had learned to live with only the barest of necessities, but from what Mick said, they were as rich in spirit as they were poor in material goods. They lived in harmony and balance with nature and with each other; they were hardy and resilient; they took great pride in their rituals and traditions; and they had a spiritual life strong enough to sustain them through all of their hardships. Surely they had much to teach us. But what would happen to them, I wondered, once they found themselves connected to the internet, to cellphone service, to movies and television, to all the changes people from the industrialized world would obviously bring with them when they found their way to this valley?

I remembered the words of Wade Davis, a modern-day Indiana Jones. He warned about the risks of cultural homogenization, which could result in the loss of thousands of years of Indigenous wisdom. It is strange that we speak with such a sense of sorrow about the disappearance of so many animal and plant species on our planet, while seeming indifferent to the danger that, in our lifetime, we are at risk of seeing half of the world's cultures disappear, and with them their languages, thoughts, stories and legacies.[1] Questions raced through my mind. What did it mean for a part of human consciousness to be gone forever? What did this mean for our future as a human race? If our differences and cultural diversity are our strengths, what would happen to us if we all become the same? What can we learn from traditional cultures that have survived the test of time – and is there time to learn it before it is all lost?

Was this why I had for so long felt drawn to Nepal and its people? This sense that there was something they had to teach me? Maybe even something I could do to help preserve those teachings for others?

My thoughts were pierced by a quote I remembered from author Steven Pressfield: "Our job in this lifetime is not to shape ourselves into some ideal we imagine we ought to be, but to find out who we already are and become it."[2] Maybe it wasn't about always driving forward but rather stopping long enough to reflect, to remember. Looking back to rediscover something we'd lost along the way.

And so, in a heartbeat, as we had done so many times before, Chantal and I created a vision for a new adventure. We would travel to the Lost Valley. We would observe and learn from an ancient Himalayan mountain people. And we would document what we learned by bringing together a new team – a team of like-minded artists with different skills. With their help, we would be able to use photography, music, art and film to capture the journey. We would witness and record a moment in time before it changed.

But that was when I saw the photo. The pyramid mountain. I grasped Mick's phone in my hands, feeling the muscles in my face tighten and my heart beat faster. Everything we had just discussed suddenly seemed secondary, for a new flame had been kindled. I tried not to reveal the excitement that now pulsated through my veins, but Chantal knew me all too well. Nothing could stop me. There was no doubt in my mind, and there was no going back. It was time for me to go to Nepal. Time to climb that mountain.

TWO

The plane landed on the cracked, bumpy runway and came to a sudden stop with an unexpected jolt. As we exited the aircraft, the thick, humid air hit us like a wave, carrying the smells of burnt garbage and diesel, with an aftertaste of sewage. Within minutes we got our first dose of Kathmandu mayhem. Since it was shortly before midnight, and there were almost no lights to illuminate the darkness, we could see little of the chaotic scene unfolding around us. A swarm of men emerged from the shadows, jostling for our bags, trying to get us to use their airport carts so they could collect money for the rental. Others hollered at us to hire their taxis. Chantal and I, along with our friends Jason and Michael, forced our way through the mob, looking for a sign from our scheduled pickup. Mick's company, Wilderness Trekking, was supposed to send a car for us. Although Mick himself had not come, he had entrusted us to his hand-picked Nepali team with whom he'd been trekking for over a decade.

One man who spoke better English than what we heard in the general cacophony singled me out from the crowd. "Sir, who are you looking for?"

"Wilderness Trekking," I called back.

The man disappeared into the crowd. A few minutes later another man appeared. He was thin and wore a black dress shirt and a tweed blazer.

"Wilderness, sir. Yes, I am Wilderness."

We muscled our way through with our duffel bags, and before we knew it a few young men had grabbed the bags and helped us all into an unmarked white van. I sat up front with the driver and the man in the tweed jacket, and our van quietly rolled away, leaving the bustle of the airport behind. Only our headlights and the glow of burning garbage lit the road-side. Peering through the darkness, we caught our first few glimpses of the city. Gaunt cows and stray dogs roamed freely. The street was rough and filled with potholes. It was hard to gain a sense of direction as we zigzagged the winding dirt roads, squeezing through alleys and around motorbikes, a variety of banged-up vehicles and the few pedestrians who were out at that late hour. At one point the street was so narrow we had to inch our way past a bus coming from the opposite direction. Only a couple of centimetres separated us from the bus on our right, while on the left the rear tire of our van protruded over the edge of the road, which over-looked a swampy garbage- and sewage-filled moat several metres below us. I couldn't help but visualize our van tumbling down the ravine into the bacteria-infested sludge. Gawd, this would be a helluva way to go.

My thoughts turned from that unwelcome prospect to the men in whose company we now found ourselves. I realized we actually had no idea if they were who they said they were.

"You know Mick?" I asked the man in the tweed jacket.

"Yes. Mick. Very good man," he replied.

"He seems to have his hands full these days with his kids. I can't recall how many he has now."

"Yes, two sons now. He just had little baby."

Of course, I was fully aware that Mick had recently had a second son, but knowing that our Nepali companion also knew this put my mind at ease. I let my vigilance lapse and allowed myself to relax until finally, after a 13-hour flight from Vancouver, a couple nights layover in Hong Kong, a five-hour flight to Kathmandu and this late-night bus ride, we arrived at our hotel – a plain brick building, three stories high, with a few potted plants out in front.

"You guys made it," came a familiar voice from a dark corner of the lobby. Our friend and expedition photographer Arek greeted us with open arms. He was taller than the rest of us but light on his feet, and his hugs were heartfelt. His kind smile and the warmth of his welcome lifted our spirits immediately. Our team was complete and together at last. After a few minutes of congratulating ourselves on having travelled the long distance to Kathmandu with no mishaps along the way, it was time for bed.

As it was late, there was no staff in evidence, except the hotel guard we'd seen at the gates on the way in. But our Nepali friend had keys for us, and Chantal and I made our way to our room, number 111, which was tucked away in a dark corner of the hotel's basement. I was so exhausted from travel that I nearly missed the smell of urine emanating from the rusted and stained toilet. Or was it coming from the shower? A single, damp, crumpled, half-roll of toilet paper sat on an otherwise empty shelf. Chantal tore back the sheets on the bed and was about to lie down when she noticed yellowish stains in the middle, along with some dark, rust-coloured spots. She touched one of the spots and it smeared. Damn. Bedbugs.

Somehow the state of our room didn't get to me. After all, despite the long odds against it, we were about to embark on the adventure we had dreamed of for so long. There had been many times during the nearly 12 months it had taken to plan and organize this expedition when we thought it was going to fall through. Everyone in our group had faced considerable challenges to make it happen. For Chantal and me, the main problem was taking the necessary time away from work. We both had clients who counted on our availability, and we'd be without mobile phone access for several weeks. On top of this, we'd both accumulated a lot of student debt while working on our master's degrees, which we'd finished only recently.

Michael, the wandering minstrel and our expedition musician, had to push very hard to raise the money to get to Nepal, which he had done, appropriately enough, through his music. On top of his marathon busking, which he needed just to get by, Michael had also raised funds by giving concerts during which he raffled off some of his instruments, as well as performances for people's house parties. When he realized this wasn't going to be nearly enough, he started an Indiegogo campaign, raced to record and release a new album and rented a theatre where he organized and performed a CD release party. It was only by the skin of his teeth that he'd managed to pull together the necessary funds a mere four weeks before we were meant to leave.

And then there was our expedition artist, Jason, a nature artist and urban cowboy biologist from Calgary. Initially, he was apprehensive about joining, as I would later discover, because he didn't feel his art was good enough. Once he finally worked up the confidence to go, he was stunned by what it was going to cost, and he decided it was impossible for him to join us. Not to mention the fact that he caught pneumonia just a few weeks before we were meant to leave – and his marriage was on the rocks. But we weren't giving up on him. In our eyes, he was a first-class artist who shared our passion for adventure and exploration. He was a critical member of our team, and we felt we would not be complete without him. The tipping point was when he saw how hard Michael was pushing with his music. Michael even offered to give him money out of whatever excess funds he was able to raise. That was enough to push the Calgarian into full gear. He began printing and distributing posters to pre-sell commissioned art – art he would create from our expedition. Before long, he had sold several paintings and had amassed enough funds to join the team.

Arek, a Polish geomatics professor and one of the most talented photographers I've ever met, had come on board relatively late in the process. In fact, it was Michael's fundraising that had brought him to us, because Arek happened to win one of Michael's home concert raffles. The two of them hit it off like childhood playmates because they both had a youthful spontaneity that kept them in high spirits most of the time. When Arek found out what Michael was raising funds for, and that the team still needed a photographer, it wasn't even a question for him. It had been Arek's dream to be the photographer on an expedition like this. He was on a research sabbatical, so he had the freedom to go. And since he had recently separated from his wife, our expedition provided the perfect opportunity for him to get away and find some perspective on the upheaval in his life.

Besides an artist, a musician and a photographer, Chantal and I had also arranged to have a filmmaker join our expedition. But only a couple of weeks before we were leaving he'd dropped out. With time so short, I decided to buy the necessary camera equipment so Chantal and I could film the journey ourselves, even though we had no idea what we were doing. But it didn't matter. Just as it didn't matter that we were now in a hole of a room that reeked of urine and was infested with bedbugs. What did matter was that we had given our all to get here, and here we were. I'd learned through the many months of planning, of stops and starts, of hopes that were continually being dashed and then raised again, that it was only by letting go of expectations that everything began to fall into place.

We were a team, united by our curiosity and openness to what lay ahead. United by the pull of the Lost Valley. It would all work out.

The next morning, as I passed the key to room 111 to the hotel concierge, his welcoming smile turned to a look of chagrin. He hadn't realized we'd spent the night in such a terrible room. Turns out the hotel had been overbooked, which is why we ended up being sent to the only bed it had left, in a filthy, unkempt spare room that wasn't even supposed to be for hotel guests. Fortunately, he upgraded us for the following night, giving us a room that, while not luxurious, was more like what we expected from a three-star hotel.

As we discovered with our room, the whole of Kathmandu was a place of extreme ups and downs, of opposites existing in an inexplicable form of organized chaos. We would get fully acquainted with those contrasts that first morning, when we made our way out into the city for a bit of exploring. If there was such a thing as sensory overload, this surely was it. The sparsely populated, dimly lit streets and caged up storefronts we had glimpsed the night before were now bustling and exploding with life. People poured into the streets and alleyways from every corner. The brick walls that lined the narrow passageways were now buried beneath an avalanche of goods for sale: clothing, bags, beads, sandals, paintings, masks, jewelry, housewares and handmade ornaments of all kinds. Motorbikes belched blue smoke at us as they wove through the obstacle course, while stunning Hindu women adorned in brightly coloured silk saris of red, yellow, green and blue glided through the narrow streets. Peddlers accosted each passerby with offers of a hodgepodge of trinkets. Animal carcasses were butchered and sold in the street, attracting clouds of flies and customers alike. Next to them sat colourful burlap sacks full to the brim with a variety of spices, grains and dried fruits. Bony cows stood still as statues in their own feces amid heaps of garbage as traffic swarmed carefully around them. Street children ran about, their dark hair matted, skin stained with dirt, clothes in tatters. Old women in hooded veils lit butter lamps and incense in the street. The incessant blowing of car and bike horns, and the ever-present rumblings of diesel engines, accompanied the sounds of small bells and distant instruments. Prayer flags fluttered. Monks chanted. Beggars pleaded. Pigeons flapped. Stray dogs slept. Dark eyes glared mysteriously. And the whole scene unfolded beneath the deep red glow of Kathmandu's morning sun, its rays dimmed by the thick cloud of polluted smoke that enshrouded the valley, blocking out the views of the majestic Himalayan ranges.

Had we been in any other place, our team might have attracted some attention, for we appeared to be a rather oddly mismatched group: Arek with his bright beaded bracelets and necklaces and painted toenails; Michael with his long golden hair wrapped in a purple bandana, a blond pointy goatee and a guitar slung over one shoulder; Jason with his thick handlebar moustache beneath the curved brim of a large brown cowboy hat; and Chantal and I, much more conventional-looking types with our sport sunglasses and high-performance, trim-fitting climbing wear. But here in the streets of Kathmandu, we were but a tiny piece of a vast spectrum of ever-moving colour and sound. We fit right in – with each other and with the scene at large.

That day we ventured for hours in our explorations, through tiny twisting alleyways and traffic-jammed streets, over rickety bridges and into imposing sacred temples. We crossed rivers that appeared as though a hundred garbage trucks had dumped their loads onto the banks that flanked them. On a wooded hilltop not far from the centre of town, we visited the ancient temple of Swayambhunath, a Buddhist holy site that now attracts crowds of pilgrims and tourists alike. Also known as the "Monkey Temple" because of the hundreds of resident monkeys cavorting amid the trees and the various temples and shrines that make up this complex, it is an extraordinary sight. Tired as we were from our long trip, we found it well worth the effort to walk up the 365 steps to the vast white dome of the stupa, crowned with a golden cube, from each side of which two giant Buddha eyes stared down at us.

Before I could become too mesmerized by those eyes, I found myself absorbed by the soft reverberations of a heavy bronze Tibetan singing bowl. Michael was tapping the edge of one, which he had purchased a few minutes before from one of the many street vendors in the temple complex. And just like that, in the middle of the pandemonium, the deep meditative hum of the singing bowl created a sliver of stillness. It was as though everyone had taken a brief pause to listen to those haunting tones.

At that moment a young monkey came over and perched beside me. His friendly face gazed up with curiosity, and I saw what looked like a sense of wonder in his eyes. "Hello friend. So, you made your way into this strange place too. You and I aren't so different, are we?"

Toward the end of the day, Chantal and I found ourselves standing before the gates of another holy site, this one the Hindu temple complex of Pashupatinath, which comprises hundreds of temples and monuments, large and small, all of them very different from Buddhist-style temples with their distinctive dome-shaped stupas topped with the eyes of Buddha. Across the river from where we stood we could see the three-story Hindu temple that is the centrepiece of the complex – its most sacred building and the only one that is not open to non-Hindus. The lower half of this temple was carved elaborately from wood, while its pagoda-style upper levels, which look like two pyramids stacked on top of each other, with a spire at the pinnacle, were made of copper covered in gold that glowed against the sky. Nothing I had ever seen had prepared me for the sight of the immense Pashupatinath complex – or for the whole experience of being there.

Death: that is why most people, besides tourists, come to Pashupatinath. Every day of the year, open-air cremations take place on the ghats leading up from the Bagmati, one of Kathmandu's major rivers. Even as we watched, five or six burning pyres on the opposite bank were casting smoke into the sky, and with the smoke rose the ashes from the incinerated flesh of the dead. Family members gazed at the cremations as the corpses went up in flames.

Below the pyres, the Bagmati, congested with debris and garbage, slowly inched its way forward. Upstream a man defecated into the river. A hundred metres downstream a family shared food and drink as they picnicked on the mucky, trash-laden bank. Young girls, pants rolled to their knees, waded barefoot in the sludge. Some had rakes, others used their bare hands, searching through the filthy mire for any trinkets of value that might have accompanied the remains once they were shovelled into the Bagmati. No doubt the river was filled with cholera, typhoid and god knows what flesh-eating or other potentially fatal bacterial diseases.

We stood there for several minutes taking it all in. The whole scene played out against the backdrop, across the river, of that magnificent, golden-roofed temple. Behind me a family of tourists appeared. The father and mother were dressed impeccably in khaki shorts, polo shirts and white sweaters draped over their shoulders. Their perfectly groomed children followed in tow. Somehow my stomach turned as they started snapping pictures of the funerals – the burning corpses, mourning families and all.

Chantal and I made our way across the bridge to the opposite side of the Bagmati. We passed the burning pyres. We passed the elderly and the sick. We passed lepers with their mangled limbs, and we passed the street children with their soft hopeful eyes. We walked up the stairs leading to the entrance of the main temple. A sign and guard at the entrance signalled that only Hindus were permitted to enter. As I stood before the entrance, someone exited, opening the intricately carved doors and revealing its interior. In that moment a waft of air carried the stench of rotting burnt flesh mixed with the feces smeared on the stairs beside me. The smell dropped me to a knee and for a moment I thought I was going to vomit all over the stairs.

As I fought to suppress my nausea, I glanced up across the temple threshold and glimpsed the shrine inside. Women and men in vivid clothing floated amid the elaborate monuments. They appeared to move almost in slow motion, their silk headscarves and loose robes flowing delicately behind them. My eyes caught those of a young boy as he emerged from behind the doorway, a look of awe on his face. He was clearly deeply moved by whatever it was he had seen inside. I felt like I was stuck between two worlds: one of death, disease, poverty and suffering; the other of life, beauty, colour, joy and transcendence.

Where was I?

Overwhelmed by it all, Chantal pleaded with me to come away. We retreated back down the stairs, past the street children, past the beggars, past the burning pyres, past the sick and the dying and the dead. Chantal broke down, tears streaming from behind her sunglasses. Kathmandu's contradictions were too much for her. And it was true that one couldn't help but be horrified by the city's contrasts, its magnificent temples and begging sadhus, the beautiful silk saris and gold jewelry on many of the women, and the rags on the street beggars, the filth in its rivers and the green of its verdant forests.

Throughout our wanderings that day, I had been stunned by the shocking state of Kathmandu. It seemed strange that a country that had essentially managed to maintain its independence for over 200 years, never having allowed the British to make it a colony (unlike its powerful neighbour, India), could become one of the poorest countries in the world.[3] How could a people so culturally strong, with so much pride, let their capital city fall into such disarray and allow so many of their fellow citizens to exist in such dire poverty?

The answers lay in part in the country's recent history. For nearly 140 years, beginning in the year 1816, under the rule of the Shah Dynasty and then the Rana Dynasty, Nepal had been a global hermit, closing its borders to the rest of the world as part of its effort to resist colonization. It wasn't until the early 1950s that it began to open them again. Though it seemed to be entering the modern world at the time, as it established relations with other countries, wrote a constitution establishing a parliamentary system of government and held its first election in 1959, this apparent stability was illusory. The decades that followed saw kings seizing power over the entire country, once in 1960 and again in 2005; a bloody Maoist insurgency that lasted a decade and cost thousands of lives; the massacre of nearly the entire royal family in 2001 by the king's son, Crown Prince Dipendra; riots in the streets, mass arrests and the rise and fall of one government after another in the aftermath of the assassination. In short, the country was living in a state of chaos, corruption and violence. The monarchy had been officially dissolved in 2008, but the existence of literally dozens of political parties competing for power did not bode well for any future hopes of internal peace and stability. At the time we were there in 2012, years of attempts to form a new constitution that reflected Nepal's emergence from monarchy to a supposed democracy were still ongoing – and in fact would not succeed until 2015.[4]

I knew some but not all of that history then, but I did know enough to be aware that the country was very tense, its political stability hanging by a thread. And as Chantal and I looked over the scene at the temple complex, unsure what to make of it all, my reactions were so complicated that I felt as though I was absorbing into my very being some of the country's turbulence.

It was time to go. The smoke and smells from the burning cremation pyres seemed to follow us on our way back to the hotel. Yet all around us life went on, beneath the amber light of Kathmandu's red sun.

THREE

After a couple of days exploring Kathmandu and making final arrangements for our expedition, we were on our way. It was early April, and we
were hoping for good weather for the month to come.

Our bus rumbled down the mountain road, leaving a cloud of dirt in
its wake. The old rust bucket had seen better days. Its bright pink paint
job, which sported a jaunty blue thunderbolt down the back, was covered in myriad dents, scratches and nicks. Its tires were also tread-worn,
which worried me a bit, especially as I watched the driver fighting violently with his stick shift. His eyes remained fixed firmly ahead at all times,
his attention never wavering for a moment, as he navigated the winding
road, making hairpin turns and dodging large rocks and potholes that
were more like sinkholes. To the left, rocky cliffs stretched vertically upwards, and a couple feet to the right the crumbling lane overlooked a deep
gorge where the great Marsyangdi River flowed along the valley bottom.
The whole bus shook back and forth, as though swaying to the sounds
of the Nepali music blaring over the vehicle's ear-piercing sound system.
Mounds of gear and provisions for the month ahead were crammed into
every available space on the bus, and another big heap was strapped to the
exterior roof. There were 19 of us in all, the five in our group plus a team
of 14, which included a cook, three kitchen boys, porters, mule drivers
and, of course, our guides, which explained why there was so much stuff.
Once we'd stowed most of our gear inside, there wasn't enough room for
all of us, so most of our crew sat atop the vehicle, as did Michael, who had
thought it would be fun – until he realized he had to hang on for dear life.

Despite being stuffed in a rickety bus, it felt good to get out of the smog and pandemonium of Kathmandu. We would begin our trek on the famous Annapurna Circuit, a high-altitude trail circumnavigating the Annapurna range. The trek became popular among tourists when it was opened to foreigners in 1977, after Nepal's government finally succeeded in removing the Khampa guerrilla fighters who had been orchestrating raids into Tibet from that area.[5] Since then, the Annapurna Circuit had become one of the most sought-after high mountain treks in the world, attracting tens of thousands of foreigners each year, who spend weeks wandering beneath some of the world's most majestic peaks. We, however, would travel only the first quarter of the circuit before branching off through a nondescript, almost hidden, keyhole gap to the north. This was our doorway into the Lost Valley.

Our driver's face finally lost its look of grim determination when, after eight hours of jarring, dusty roads, the road petered out into a dirt path, and the rocky cliffs yielded to lush, green, forested hillsides. We had arrived at the peaceful farming community of Bhulbhule. A grey mist drifted over Bhulbhule's rice paddies and through the leaves of the trees that were scattered among its tin-roofed farmhouses and pastures. We would rest here for the night and start our journey on foot in the morning.

We set up camp in a farmer's field just north of the small settlement and were instantly swarmed by an excited crowd of local children. Most of them were little girls, and they looked especially excited to see Chantal. When Chantal introduced herself as "Shanti," one of the girls screamed with glee. It was nearly impossible for Nepalis to pronounce Chantal's name, so she had decided to call herself "Shanti" while in Nepal, which was actually a nickname I had begun calling her when we were first dating. Unbeknownst to us at that time, "Shanti" is a common Nepali name meaning "peace." The girls took Chantal by her hand, bringing her to another little girl – who was also named Shanti. The fact that Chantal had a name that was the same as one of theirs was a source of great amusement to them. Soon they were climbing all over Chantal, hanging from her back, swinging from her arms and holding her hands. Chantal responded with delight. The heavy-heartedness that had weighed her down the previous days in Kathmandu was dissipating, giving way to the joy she felt at being in this beautiful place and in the company of these high-spirited children. Her eyes lit up, and the smile I had fallen in love with replaced the tight-lipped expression she'd worn since the burning pyres of Pashupatinath.

I knew Chantal had felt in her own heart the suffering of many of those she saw in Kathmandu. She had fought to let it go but had been unable to shake it off until now. From the moment I met Chantal, I had recognized her extreme sensitivity. I'd never known someone who cared so deeply for all other living beings, and I knew she was struggling with the vast dichotomies of this country. But as she was beginning to discover, Nepal was a place of opposites. If one was open to it, there was an abundance of joy and beauty to be found in the most unlikely of places.

I surveyed the hills before us. They spanned outward to the north, and over the coming days our path would weave through them. Ever gaining ground, going ever deeper. A string of colourful prayer flags floated in the evening breeze above our camp. They reminded me of the ones I had seen on the cover of the Lonely Planet book my sister had given me those many years ago. It seemed odd to be standing here – as if I was now living between the covers of the book I had loved so much as a teenager.

It may have taken me 15 years, but I had finally arrived, and I felt ready for whatever awaited me. I was excited about our plan to document and pay tribute to the heritage of the villages of the Lost Valley. Yet, in the weeks to come, whatever ideas I had about what we had to offer this land would be dwarfed by what it would bring to us.

We said goodbye to our driver, and for the next several days we followed the well-trodden dusty trail, making our way north by northwest into the mountains. We journeyed through the villages like a motley posse, passing tea houses whose owners made their living by providing food and lodging for the trekkers on the Annapurna Circuit. Surrounded by little white fences, small patches of manicured grasses and beautiful flowers, many of the houses looked straight out of a fairy tale – an oddly anomalous sight amid the worn down, tin-roofed houses of the villagers. Michael strummed his guitar as we walked beneath thousands of terraced rice paddies that climbed the hillsides like stairs. Nepali boys ran behind us as we left each village, pleading for Michael to play one more song for them. "Michael Jackson! Michael Jackson!"

Women dressed in brilliantly coloured clothing hacked at the grasses and soil with their hand tools, while old men sat hunched on the steps of their houses, staring into space. We strode past stone gates and sunbathing dogs. We passed spinning brass prayer wheels and colourful prayer flags. White-maned monkeys peered down at us from the trees as we crossed countless steel-and-wire-mesh hanging bridges spanning deep gorges. We trod under waterfalls and over heaps of mule dung. We watched a woman decapitate and butcher a goat with an axe, and averted our eyes at the sight of a mule being held down by seven men while it was castrated – its cry could be heard for half a mile. Bright-eyed children never failed to appear, each more adorable than the one before, greeting us always with a welcoming "Namaste-eeee," their hands pressed firmly together. And everywhere we went the deep red buds of the rhododendron, Nepal's national flower, slowly opened their petals to the warmth of the spring sun, decorating the trail around us.

I spent much of my time on the trail with Dawa, a Sherpa who was one of the more experienced members of our crew. Dawa was older than the others, small in stature and stoutly built, but he carried himself lightly on the trail and had an outsized zest for life that I admired. For some reason unknown to me, I felt a strong affinity to the Sherpa, one of Nepal's hundred-plus ethnic groups, most of whom lived in the northeastern part of Nepal. Their religion and traditions are similar to those of the Tibetan Buddhists, and as I asked Dawa about his people and their culture, it soon became evident that his knowledge of Tibetan Buddhism ran deep. He seemed to take a real interest in my questions, and was eager to share what he knew about both Sherpa culture and Buddhist philosophy. I felt myself growing closer to him as we walked.

Before long, we entered a small settlement called Bagarchhap. Arek, Michael and Jason had congregated around what appeared to be some kind of partition made of rocks in the middle of the trail. I eased my pack off my shoulder and placed it on the rocks, ready to take a short break.

It was no mere stack of rocks. "This is memorial to a village buried some years ago by a landslide," Dawa said. He remembered when it happened, and explained that Bagarchhap had once had many more buildings than it did now.

I examined the area around us. It was hard to believe that a landslide had wiped out most of this village, burying locals and trekkers alike. Surveying the surrounding hills, a habit I had adopted over time to anticipate hazards in the mountains, I could see no sign of being in a high-risk area. But that was the nature of the Himalaya. The dangers were often triggered much higher up and out of sight. The victims here would never have known what was coming for them – until it was too late.

Amid the weather-beaten buildings and the hazy grey skies, the colours of the ever-present prayer flags shone brightly. Dawa had explained to me that each colour represented one of the five elements. "Life is good when all elements in balance," he would say. He also told me about the Tibetan mantras embedded into the cloth. As the wind blew the flags, it would carry the auspicious mantras forward, sending them out into the world to help spread peace and compassion.

Nearby we could hear a little girl's laughter. The girl was pointing at Jason's thick handlebar moustache, showing it to her younger brother. She was amused by it, drawing her fingers beneath her own nose and down to her chin, giggling at the Calgarian cowboy. Wherever we went, villagers were fascinated by Jason's moustache, examining it closely as if it were a unique ethnic or cultural phenomenon. Jason, looking up from his sketchbook, contorted his face into a grimace. "Isn't this the most disgusting moustache you've ever seen?" he called out as the children ran away laughing.

We soon left Bagarchhap behind, as we had many other villages, continuing along the wandering trail, much of which passed through the backyards of farmers and their harvest fields. The higher we climbed, the more mani walls and chortens we encountered. Dawa explained that we must walk clockwise around them to show respect for Buddha, and also because it was the way the sun travelled across the sky. I lost count of how many we passed. Most of the walls housed prayer wheels, inscribed with the Tibetan mantra "*om mani padme hum*," repeated over and over again.

"What does it mean?" I asked Dawa, hopeful he would be able to enlighten me, since no one I had asked so far had been able to explain the mantra. Clearly, the words had some kind of profound significance, for they appeared in so many places, but the mystery of their meaning seemed to be too deep for anyone to unravel.

"Wait for Lama at Tashi gompa," was Dawa's response. He was referring to the lama who was stationed at the Tashi Lhakhang monastery, who was said to be a wise man. Tashi Lhakhang was a hilltop monastery perched to the north of Phu village, and one of the most isolated monasteries in all of Nepal. Phu, a medieval settlement that was a mere two-day trek from the Tibetan border, was the most remote outpost in the Lost Valley. It was our team's final destination – the place from which I was hoping to set out in search of the pyramid mountain.

We were still several days away from Phu, but apparently I would have to wait until we got there for my answer. For the moment, there seemed to be nothing else to say, so we continued walking in silence. Yet, being the outgoing man he was, it wasn't long before Dawa engaged me in conversation again.

"Maike, do you want to climb Mount Everest?"

"At one time, yes, I did."

"And now you do not?"

"I realized I did not want to climb it for me. I wanted to climb it because of what others would think. But now I no longer climb for others to see me."

The topic of Everest troubled me. Everest is sacred to the Sherpa community that lives in its foothills. So much so that, until Western tourists arrived, they didn't climb it, for fear of offending *Chomolungma*, as they refer to it, which means "Goddess Mother of the Land" in Tibetan. I had tremendous respect for the mountain, yet the fact that it had been turned into a tourist industry, that hundreds of inexperienced foreigners flocked to its slopes each year, that this mountain was being exploited simply because of its being the highest in the world, rubbed me the wrong way. It seemed to me that the Sherpas were being exploited too, for it would have been impossible for these people to climb the mountain without the help of the Sherpas. It is very lucrative work for them – not by our standards, but by those of their peers. According to an article in the *Washington Post*, "a lead mountain guide earns as much as $6,000 during the three-month climbing season. The monthly average salary of Nepalis is $48." But the work is also extremely dangerous. According to that same article, when ranked by annual fatality rates per profession, it is also regarded as the most dangerous profession in the world.[6]

Is it right for so many Sherpas to risk and even lose their lives to the mountain, for the sole purpose of earning money from foreign novices eager to make their way up so they can tell their tales of climbing the world's highest mountain? Is it right to commoditize the experience of climbing Everest? Of course, I understood that mountain tourism was a critical part of Nepal's shaky economy. But perhaps the whole thing didn't sit well with me because it seemed like such a microcosm of our modern world, with those who have money being able to buy extreme experiences at the expense of those who do not.

And perhaps it made me uneasy because I, myself, with my team of 14 Nepalis, was complicit. I wasn't climbing Everest, of course, but I had my eyes on another mountain, and who knew what dangers it would present? My plan was to leave my companions behind in Phu for the week we had allotted to documenting its culture, while I went off with a couple of the guides to find and, if possible, scale the pyramid mountain. Afterwards, I would rendezvous with the group in Nar, a village in a valley adjacent to Phu, where we were supposed to have a brief stopover, or back in Kathmandu, if there wasn't enough time for me to get to Nar.

"What do you think about climbing Everest?" I asked Dawa.

Dawa grew excited. "This is great goal for many Sherpa people – to have the chance to climb Everest. Many of my friends also want to have chance to climb Everest. It is big honour. Very good money."

And there I had it. I felt saddened by Dawa's response. Yet judging Dawa's words through my Western filter wasn't fair. There was no simple answer. For the exploitation of something sacred, many people in Nepal were benefitting. What would I do if I were in their shoes? Was it right for me to judge them for seizing their chance to get ahead in one of the poorest countries in the world? Was it even right for me to judge the tourists who gave them that chance?

"Why do *you* climb, Maike?" Dawa asked, his eyes meeting mine.

Usually, I would have brushed that question off with some kind of flippant remark. But under the circumstances, Dawa's question demanded an answer, and I knew I had to say something. It took me awhile to formulate a response, however, because the question stirred up so many thoughts and such powerful memories. Truth be told, I wasn't always obsessed with mountains, or even much interested in nature. For most of my high school days, I played the electric guitar in a rock band, wore my hair long past my shoulders, hung out with a bunch of guys who did the same and worked on my kitchenware business. When I was 17, however, my dad took me to a place called Carmanah Valley, home to some of the oldest, tallest trees in the world, dating back over 1,000 years and measuring over 90 metres in height. The area was later saved from logging by a handful of activists who literally chained themselves to the trees in the 1990s. To this day, it is one of the most magical places I have ever been. Carmanah changed the way I saw myself. Carmanah changed my life. And Carmanah changed my relationship with nature. After that, nature became my classroom. Nature became my sanctuary. And, in my mind, I became nature.

The trip I took with my dad when I was 17 introduced me to my love for nature. A man named Joe introduced me to my love for the mountains. When I met him, around my 18th birthday, Joe had just returned from Nepal, and since by then I had already fallen in love with Nepal, without ever having been there, I was eager to learn from him. To a kid my age, Joe seemed almost larger than life. He had travelled widely. He was a hunter and an outdoorsman. He was a mountaineer. He could shoot a cougar while rappelling down a cliff with a rifle in one hand and a rope in the other – and he could reset his own dislocated shoulder after falling down the mountainside.

One day Joe told me he wanted to take me up a mountain. I had no idea what that meant. But it sounded awesome, so I was game. Joe loaned me an ice axe, a pair of crampons and a harness, and off we went in his 4x4 pickup into the mountains. We started hiking with our head torches around 4:00 a.m. – an "Alpine start," as it's known in mountaineering. It was a cool morning and I remember feeling the dampness of the west coast rainforest. We hiked for hours, climbing through the trees, falling to all fours at times and digging our hands and boots into the frozen dirt. Elk gazed at us through the thick foliage. Eventually, we hit snow as we emerged from the subalpine and waded our way uphill through thigh-deep powder. Breaking the trail was exhausting work, but I didn't mind since it was opening a new world for me. In other words, I was loving it. When the sun rose, it began to light up the snow, which turned our surroundings into a pristine blanket of stardust.

The terrain became steeper, and the snow became firmer, until we found ourselves clambering up a 45-degree slope. We took out our ice axes, strapped on our crampons and Joe showed me what to do. Moving silently up the mountain, we kicked our front points and plunged our ice axes into the icy snow. "If you fall, dig in with the pointy end of the axe," Joe called to me as we kept kicking. Kick, kick with the right foot. Kick, kick with the left foot. Plunge the axe. Repeat. My legs were taxed and beginning to cramp. All I could think about was trying not to fall. By now we'd been moving practically nonstop for over four hours, though occasionally I had to call a time out to catch my breath.

The sun was cresting over the ridgeline and creating a halo around Joe as we approached the summit. I had been so consumed by the mechanics of the climb that I had paid little attention to how high we had gone. I looked in both directions. All I could see were perfectly undisturbed slopes of white. One side dropped off into an untold depth as the slope ended with a large corniced overhang. I looked over my right shoulder, back behind me and down to the valley from where we'd come. The sun lit up the horizon in a fiery glow, revealing countless peaks – peaks I had never seen before. Peaks I had no idea even existed. In that moment, a whole new realm of possibility had just opened. High above our everyday life, out of sight, there was another world, sculpted before any human had ever walked the earth, and accessible only by our will to climb. I could feel tears welling in my eyes, for in that moment I had found my passion. I had found myself.

For the next five years, Joe and I climbed many mountains – the biggest mountain we ever climbed together was Mount Assiniboine, often called the Matterhorn of the Canadian Rockies. We also made several forays to a rock-climbing mecca called the Bugaboos, an otherworldly mountain range west of the Canadian Rockies consisting of a series of granite rock spires shooting hundreds of metres straight up from the earth. We climbed in the North Cascades, and up and down the coastal ranges of British Columbia. Eventually, Joe nailed his climbing boots to the wall to save his marriage, and we never climbed another mountain together again. But those years climbing with Joe were some of my best.

Joe wasn't religious, but he was deeply spiritual. He once said to me, "It's better to be in the mountains thinking about god, than to be in church thinking about the mountains." Those words were in my mind when I finally answered Dawa.

"When I am climbing, the mountain is part of me, and I am part of it," I said to him. "Without the mountain, I could not exist." And I meant it. Call it spiritual. Call it being closer to god. Whatever it was, in the mountains I felt in touch with deeper truths about myself and about my place in the world. Once I felt that connection, I could no longer live without it.

I caught a gleam in Dawa's dark eyes and thought perhaps he felt something similar. We walked for some time together in the shadow of the snow-capped peaks around us, saying little. I marvelled at them. They reminded me of the Canadian Rockies back home. "What are the names of these mountains?" I asked Dawa as I gazed curiously up at them. Dawa looked back with a barely suppressed grin. "These are not mountains. These are foothills."

FOUR

The clamour of Tibetan horns, drums and cymbals broke the evening calm, erupting into a sound that can only be likened to the random blowing of bagpipes accompanied by the clashing of heavy metal drums. Chantal, Arek and I were tending to a young monk when the cacophony began to echo from a nearby building. Wearing only a robe and sandals, the monk had come to us for aid. He was delirious and shivering violently with signs of hypothermia.

It was five days into our trek and that afternoon we had reached the small village of Koto, at 2600 metres in elevation. We had ascended over 1800 metres since setting out on foot, much of which we had gained just in the previous two days. The evenings were getting colder, dusting the ground with frost, and the air began to smell of winter. Temperatures up here were deceiving – hot during the day and dropping below freezing after sunset. Koto would be our last stop along the Annapurna Circuit. Tomorrow we would branch sharply north through the narrow keyhole, making our way into the Lost Valley.

The young monk was one of many monks and nuns we'd seen on a pilgrimage heading northwest, circumnavigating the north side of the Annapurna massif. They travelled in groups, their maroon robes coalescing together into dark red waves. One of those waves, an assemblage of nuns, had enveloped us on the trail that morning, attracted by the music Michael was making. It began with Michael plucking at his guitar and tapping out a beat on its body as we walked. Soon the nuns were among us, having taken an interest in the strange-looking minstrel. And then, to their surprise, the golden-haired musician broke into a Nepali song he had composed with the help of a man who owned a Tibetan singing bowl shop near our hotel in Kathmandu.

> *Satyaaa* (truth)
> *Shanta dimag* (peaceful mind)
> *Lakshyaaa* (purpose in life)
> *Atma bishwas* (self-confidence)

A young woman named Nishta, who walked beside Michael, spontaneously joined in. To everyone's amazement, she caught onto the rhythm and words right away. Her voice was beautiful and melodious, and together they reverberated as one – a choral fusion of East and West. Guitar strings echoed. Words flowed. Harmonies danced. And, to the sound of music, we wound our way up the mountain switchbacks amid a sea of maroon robes and bare-headed women, all beneath the dominating walls of the Annapurna giants.

Never in my life had I seen such an enormous wall of snow, ice and rock. At first, I thought I was looking at a wisp of cloud in the sky, until closer inspection revealed that what loomed above us in the hazy greyness of the morning sky was actually a fragment of a broken-up glaciated ridgeline. My mind took a moment to process what I was seeing, as if it was incomprehensible that part of a mountain could be that high. Before long, the Annapurna massif opened up ahead of us. It hosted a collection of some of the most dangerous peaks in the world,[7] including one of the 14 8000-metre-high peaks – Annapurna I. Since its first ascent in 1950, the mountain has seen fewer than 200 successful ascents (versus some 4,000 who have climbed Everest), and for every three who'd climbed the mountain, one had perished trying.[8] It was an impressive range of peaks if ever I'd seen one, and were my home country's Canadian Rockies to be magically transported and set down in front of them, the Annapurna mountains would have cast their shadow over the entire range. I now understood why Dawa had referred to the mountains we saw over the previous days as "foothills."

I felt a strange sense of calm and reverence travelling with the nuns in this dramatic, otherworldly landscape. Time and space seemed to move more fluidly in their presence. Their sudden appearance in our midst gave me the sense that events would unfold as they were meant to, however unexpected they might be. When we said goodbye to them, I was grateful for the time we'd been able to share, for the serendipity of our meeting.

And now something else was drawing us. When we heard the eruption of Tibetan instruments in Koto, we didn't think twice about heading into the streets to find them. We had just finished wrapping the young monk in Arek's down jacket and beanie, which Arek had graciously offered him for the night. Chantal was ministering to the young monk with hot tea and heavy doses of our vitamin C, so she decided to stay with him while Arek, Jason and I, like giddy children, ran into the night.

About 45 metres up Koto's main pathway, we found the building where the monks who were making the noise had gathered. They were all squeezed together in one room, which had the doors and windows open to allow the sound to carry. Had we been anywhere else, this eruption of sound – the blowing of Tibetan trumpets, the clashing of cymbals and the pounding of the deep Tibetan drums – would have felt like an assault on our ears. Here in the Himalaya, however, it captured my soul. A woman welcomed us, informing us there was a larger gathering of monks at the village monastery further down the street, so we ventured onwards. Near the monastery was a longhouse of sorts; some kind of gathering place for the village. Outside its main entrance was a young man with a gentle smile, wearing trim-fitting jeans, thick-framed glasses and a black jacket. "Come in, come in," the young man ushered us in and out of the cold.

We entered the longhouse to find many monks sitting on the floor with their backs to the wall. The young man motioned to several empty cushions where we were to sit and then sat down next to us.

"My name is Sonam Dorje," he said in a heavy Tibetan accent. Sonam Dorje, we discovered, was from Phu – the very place we were heading. He was 21 years old, and had left Phu when he was 14 to study Tibetan philosophy in India. This would be his first trip back home since he had left. Seven years it had been since he had seen his village. Seven years since he had seen his parents. And our paths happened to cross at that exact moment. It was another happy accident (they seemed to be accumulating).

A kind-faced woman approached and served us each a warm cup of butter tea. I had heard about the traditional Tibetan concoction of yak butter mixed with tea leaves and salt, but this was my first taste of it. It took quite an effort to drink that thick liquid. Trying not to offend my hosts, I closed my eyes, opened my throat and downed the salty sourness as fast as I could, only to discover it is customary for Tibetans to refill their guest's cup to the brim as soon as it is empty. The woman serving the tea promptly replenished my cup, looking delighted at my apparent enjoyment of the drink. I tried to appear grateful – perhaps not entirely successfully, because Jason, who had the good sense to nurse his own cup with extreme slowness, nearly cracked up when he saw the expression on my face. Meanwhile, Arek was eagerly lapping up his drink. It must have been his Polish taste buds.

Sonam Dorje looked lost within himself. "I think I have forgotten how to speak my village language."

"Is it not similar to Tibetan?" I asked.

"Yes, like Tibetan, but very different. Phu village has own language."

As I would learn, the Bhotiya people, who were of Tibetan heritage, predominantly occupied the mountainous regions in the north. Their languages were all derived from Tibetan, but because the mountains separated the communities from each other, each area had developed its own dialect.

"How did your parents send you to India?" Jason asked. "Was your education expensive?"

"Yes, it was very expensive. My parents send me with anything they had saved. But it wasn't very much. I had to work very hard to make money and pay for education and living. I didn't tell my parents I had to work though. They would have worried too much."

I gazed into the milky fluid swirling around in my cup, pondering Sonam Dorje's words. How ironic that a 14-year-old boy, born in a village cut off from the rest of the world, would have to leave his family and venture hundreds of kilometres south, crossing all of Nepal and making his way into India, in order to get an education that would foster his Tibetan Buddhist heritage – when Tibet itself lay a mere 20 kilometres to the north of Phu. Of course, Tibet was now part of China, and it would have been hard for Sonam to go there – and once there he might not have been able to leave. I wondered about the other children from Sonam Dorje's village. If he had to travel that far for his education, and his parents had to sacrifice everything they had to make it possible, what hope could there be for the other children of the Lost Valley?

I downed the last of my butter tea, feeling the thick sour liquid pass into my stomach, trying not to grimace. Once the taste had dissipated enough that I was able to focus on something else, I thought about home, and how far we had come to be here. Of course, I would be back home and able to see my family again in a matter of weeks, unlike Sonam, who had left his family when he was just a boy, without knowing when or even if he would ever see them again. Trying to imagine what that would be like, I glanced at Sonam and our eyes met. "Did you miss Phu?" I asked him. He must have sensed the direction of my thoughts, as his gaze seemed to soften and he answered quickly.

"Yes, I missed Phu." Looking down at the floor, he went on. "I miss my mother. She is very old now. I don't even know if I will recognize her. It has been long, long time."

FIVE

Early the next morning, on a bright clear day, we left the bustling Annapurna trail behind, branching off into the narrow valley to the north. Soon we came to an old sign announcing that the Nar Phu valley is restricted to groups with special permits only – permits we had already cleared in Kathmandu.

It truly was a hidden valley, separated from the rest of the world and easily missed except for the cleft in the mountainside that created a gap not more than a hundred metres wide through which we'd entered. Whereas before we had been trekking through small villages past rows of little shops and tea houses, and through people's farms and backyards, all that was behind us now. The copious amounts of litter we had seen along the Annapurna Circuit had vanished, as had the occasional trekkers we had encountered over the previous few days. There was scarcely any sign of life. It was clear we were on our own from here on in.

Soon what was once a wide trail petered out into a thin footpath. As we climbed, we gained elevation quickly and our surroundings changed just as rapidly. Stunted mountain fir and pine grew in dense thickets in the valley, which was bounded on two sides by sheer rocky faces that rose steeply, and abruptly, from below. The trees and undergrowth looked pristine and the forest seemed somehow more alive. Clear glacier-fed water from the Nar River rushed beneath us as we zigzagged our way up the gorge.

When the cliffs became too steep to support a trail, we would cross from one bank to the other, using the countless steel and wire suspension bridges that connected the east and west sides of the river. Some of the bridges were badly damaged and were missing their metal footplates, exposing wide gaps that opened to the rapids below. Further upstream, the fresh carcass of a horse lay in the river, its leg obviously broken and eyes staring empty to the sky. It must have slipped off the cliffside trail. Its body was left where it had fallen onto the rocks, as if to signal we had entered a place where life and death balanced on the edge of a chasm.

We broke midday for lunch in a small wooded area called Dharamshala, which basically consisted of an old hollow shelter made of stacked stone. The area hardly warranted its own name – much less such an imposing one. Nonetheless, it was a good place to rest and it would be our final stop before pushing on to the small settlement of Meta. Beside a rock wall we spotted an elderly woman who was curled up in the dirt taking a nap, her head resting on a stone. She was the first person we had seen all day. The woman stirred as we neared. Her face was weathered and cracked. She wore gold, hooped earrings, a white shawl and a traditional heavy wool dress. A necklace with two coral stones and a large chunk of turquoise half the size of a fist hung around her neck. The rest of her belongings were wrapped in a bedsheet slung over one shoulder.

With no sign of alarm at our presence, she sat down next to Chantal, and with a warm smile pointed at Chantal and then to herself, as if to acknowledge they were both women. As Chantal took her hat off and let her hair down, the old woman did the same, removing a small comb from the breast of her sweater, which she used to comb through her white-streaked black hair. It was much longer than it had seemed, bundled up under her head scarf. She touched Chantal's hand, looking back to her own hands somewhat despondently, as if to compare Chantal's fair soft hands to her own, weathered and cracked from a lifetime of hard work in the mountains. Chantal gestured back to the old woman with respect and a gentle smile. A look of wonderment shone from Chantal's eyes, as if a thousand thoughts were passing through her mind. The woman spoke her own village dialect, so it was hard for the Nepalis in our group to communicate with her, although we did gather that she was from the village of Nar, a larger settlement to the west in an adjacent valley. She was on a two-day journey to visit her daughter in Meta.

Out here there were no means of communication. No electricity. No phones. Connections could be maintained only by travelling on foot, and it would take several days to hike between the villages, often over high mountain passes. As we departed, I wondered if I would ever see this woman again. I realized we hadn't even asked her for her name.

We plodded onwards for several hours, snaking our way higher along the cliffside trail. Eventually, the trail steepened, rising abruptly out of the ravine. We ascended the rocky hillside as threatening clouds began to form overhead, darkening the skies and blocking out the warmth of the sun. Mountain winds rustled the trees as cool gusts of wind blew down the valley from above. It felt like a torrential downpour would soon be upon us. A Himalayan griffon – a type of vulture native to Nepal, with a wingspan that can approach three metres – circled above, its wings fully extended as it flew northbound, seeming to signal to us the way ahead.

Chantal's pace slowed dramatically as the day grew darker, and she began to fall far behind the team. Concerned about her, I fell back too, in order to keep her within eyesight. But Arek, Jason and Michael were so far ahead of us that they had disappeared. "We have to keep moving!" I called out to her.

She kept trudging slowly up the steepening switchbacks, her steps slowing, falling ever further behind. I could see that something wasn't right, but my focus remained on the trail before us, along with the foreboding skies and the griffon soaring above. "Chantal, keep moving!" I called again. But she didn't move, and instead sat down on the nearest rock, as though her legs had simply given way. I came back down the trail toward her. A look of despair was on her face. Despite the majesty of our surroundings and the hours we had spent hiking amid the natural beauty of the forests and the streams, she seemed to have turned inward, to be wrestling with something that troubled her. The delight she had felt during the encounter with the old woman from Nar had vanished.

"Chantal, the weather is changing and we have to get to Meta before nightfall."

"What are we doing here?"

I was taken aback by the question, unsure how to answer. "Look around us," I said, waving my hands at the mountains as I tried to point out the obvious. "It's magnificent here – we're in a place few have ever been. We're in the *Himalaya*!"

Chantal's gaze turned upwards, searching through the dense trees and the whirling clouds, but for what I didn't know.

"Please, help me find it."

There was a heaviness in her voice and a weariness settling over her features that worried me. I had seen this look of despair on her before. It usually set in before a migraine attack, when she would have to lie down, sometimes for hours or even days. But this was no place to linger.

"Hon, it's not far now. We're so close. It's just above that rise. We can rest when we get to camp. We have to move now."

Chantal dutifully shouldered her pack and began to drag herself up the switchbacked trail again. I knew the settlement of Meta was less than an hour away now, and I hoped that if we could just get to camp before the rains did, all would be well with Chantal.

We ascended ever higher. The more ground we gained, the wider the valley became, until eventually the trail began to flatten. As we crested the hillside, an immense mountain revealed itself to us. IC, one of our Nepali climbing guides, pointed to the near 7000-metre peak: "Kang Guru Himal." Dark clouds whirled around it, blocking out all but its lower snow-covered flanks.

"Very dangerous mountain," he said. "Big avalanche killed entire expedition from France, as well as Sherpas. Eighteen died in one avalanche."

An eerie sensation passed through my body. For a moment I couldn't help questioning the wisdom of my plan to climb the beautiful mountain I'd seen in Mick's photos. But I put such thoughts aside. For now the only goal was to get to Meta while Chantal was still able to keep walking.

The Kang Guru Mountain fed a crumbling glacier that twisted its way down toward a small plateau overlooking the canyon. And there, at last, much to my relief, we found the small village of Meta. Other than a few shrubby juniper bushes dotted about on the hillsides of the plateau, it was bereft of vegetation, and its weathered stone buildings blended into the stark landscape around it. The winds blew off the mountain's glacier, chilling the back of my neck. As we approached the settlement, we could hear the clanging bells and neighing sounds of woolly mountain goats. After getting Chantal settled into our modest room in a lone tea house, I set off with Dawa, Michael, Jason and Arek to investigate the village.

The caretaker of the tea house, what at first seemed to be the only habitable structure around, invited us in out of the cold for some tea, where we found a few other locals huddled around the wood-burning stove. Most of the other structures we saw nearby were simply the remnants of stone walls, without roofs, and empty inside. With Dawa translating, the owner of the tea house explained that most of Meta's inhabitants had vanished long ago, though no one seemed certain of why. Some believed the original settlers of Meta had perished in an avalanche coming off Kang Guru Mountain, wiping out the entire village. Others speculated they had all died in a pandemic. Now the few intact structures that remained were mainly used as winter residences for some of the people from the neighbouring village of Nar. The mountain people of the Lost Valley were semi-nomadic, moving with the seasons, our host explained, and Meta was one of several settlements on their yearly circuit.

As our group joined the locals at a table set up in front of the wood-burning stove, dark shadows danced against the stone walls and the flickering firelight illuminated their weathered faces – faces that showed the toll taken by the harsh environment they lived in. But they welcomed us to their table as though we were family, smiling, gesturing, somehow making us feel at home, even though they spoke not a word of English. This was perhaps the starkest, most inhospitable place I'd ever visited. Yet these were some of the most hospitable people I'd ever met. Being with them felt like being with brothers and sisters from another world. It didn't matter that we didn't know each other's language – the people here spoke with their eyes.

Time seemed to be nonexistent here, and moments flowed freely from one to the next. But suddenly I thought about Chantal. I'd left her resting in our room, and I realized I should check on her to make sure she was all right. I found her curled up in her sleeping bag, tossing to and fro, rocked by the pain of her migraine, which was attacking her full force. Her shoulders and neck were rigid with tension; her whole body was crashing. I'd seen her like this before, and I knew that usually the only remedy was for her to rest in bed, and in total darkness, sometimes for up to two days. Yet this time it was clear something else was going on. She wasn't just physically ill; she was under severe mental stress.

"This trip is too much for me." Her voice was weak, and tears traced her cheeks. It hurt me to see her suffering like this, and I wasn't sure why this was happening. We'd climbed some major mountains together, and I knew how mentally and physically strong she was. The only thing I knew to do was to try to console her, for we were far from any help. I told her we would take it slowly tomorrow, and that we could take a rest day in Kyang, our next destination.

"This is your journey, Mike. Not mine," she whispered. I helped her sit up. Her whole body was shaking and she was extremely weak. Each movement seemed to require great effort. She let her head fall to my shoulder. I gently rubbed her neck and shoulders, feeling how rock-hard the muscles had become. It was as though every muscle along her spine had seized up into knots.

"Let's get some dinner." I tried to sound optimistic and hopeful. "A hot meal and some tea will make you feel better. One of the locals is making yak stew."

"Stew would make me vomit right now." She wrapped her arms around herself. I could hear a slight wheeze in her chest as she breathed. "Tea and broth maybe."

I helped Chantal get to her feet, and we began to make our way over to the tea house. She could barely stand upright, and I had to support her as we walked, taking each step very slowly. At the threshold to the tea house, Chantal turned to me: "Mike, I have to tell you. I think I can muster enough strength to get to Kyang, but beyond that I think I'll have to turn around."

This announcement caught me off guard. I was unsure of how to react. Of course, I was concerned about Chantal, but the thought of aborting the journey was terrible. This was everything I'd dreamed of – the place I'd wanted to be for what seemed like my entire life. I was practically vibrating with the energy of this place, the people we'd met, the landscapes we'd passed through, the very air we breathed. And the pyramid mountain – how could I leave before I even got to see it?

My thoughts turned to the others. Michael and Jason had put a lot on the line to be here. I knew Michael had literally emptied his bank account of every cent he had. He had also made a personal commitment to his Indiegogo supporters. Jason, too, had commitments to meet. To finance his trip, he'd taken advance commissions for several pieces of art, which he would have to present upon his return. Arek seemed pretty dead set on getting to Phu as well. And now all of it was at risk of falling apart.

Even though Chantal insisted she could go back with one of our Sherpas, there was no way I was going to let her return without me. That wasn't an option as far as I was concerned. But I didn't know where that would leave the rest of the team. Thoughts raced through my head as I tried to play out all the possible scenarios. How was I going to break the news to the team? How would they respond? How would we carve up all our resources if Chantal and I turned back but they decided to push on? My insides were twisting. Partly from frustration and even anger, partly from trying to empathize with the pain Chantal was going through.

The evening winds pulled my gaze to the north – our intended direction for tomorrow's trek. Above us the Himalayan griffon was still circling. Riding an airstream with its wings stretched out, motionless, it spiralled steadily upwards. Round and round, higher and higher. Until all of a sudden it broke free of the current, plummeting toward the earth. And, in a brief moment, it had dropped behind the ridgeline and was gone.

SIX

Chantal was able to sleep through the night, and had a modest appetite over breakfast the next day. Although her energy was still precariously low, I felt she would be able to make it to the settlement of Kyang, which was only half a day's trek from where we were.

Pushing on that morning, we continued to circumnavigate northward to the west side of Kang Guru Mountain. It had been two days since we'd branched off into the Lost Valley, and in that time we had gained 1200 metres, which brought us to 3800 metres above sea level. At that height we were beginning to feel the effects of the thinner air. Now it wasn't just Chantal who was lagging behind, but Jason too – to the point where the young Sherpas had nicknamed him "Junge Baaje," literally translating as "bearded grandpa." I slowed our pace so we could conserve our strength.

I was particularly worried about Chantal, who was still suffering from a severe migraine, as well as from the pain in her neck and shoulders. If anything, her symptoms were getting worse. She kept her sunglasses on even though it was cloudy. The pain forced her to dose herself heavily with sumatriptan, the prescription drug she took for migraines, but it seemed to have little effect, other than making her delirious. I made sure to stay close to her as she stumbled along. At times I would notice her face turned skyward, as if desperately searching for strength from the radiance of the majestic mountains around us. I knew she was hanging on by a thread, her energies waning with every step, and I feared she would indeed decide to turn back after we got to Kyang.

I hadn't told any of the others about how bad she was, and I certainly hadn't told anyone how close we were to having to turn around. Devi, the team sirdar (the leader of our Nepali crew), watched us warily, as though he suspected something wasn't right, but he was too polite to pry. Trying not to think about what was beginning to seem inevitable, I kept my mind on the path ahead of me. Back home I'd always found guidance in the mountains. Yet in this moment they were silent, except for the howling of the wind.

Before long, a small settlement of stone houses came into view, nestled at the base of a major rock face. We had reached the old Khampa settlement of Kyang. Coming upon this tiny settlement hidden amid such dominating walls seemed surreal. The Phu River flowed around it to the west, and the Mruju River flanked the settlement to the south, before the rivers joined, becoming one.

We'd been told the Khampas had seized these areas from the locals in Nar and Phu decades before, in the 1960s, and had used them as staging grounds for their raids into Tibet, where they were trying to reclaim the lands that the Chinese invaders had stolen from them. The local villagers, a handful of farmers and herders, wouldn't have been able to stand up to the mighty Khampa warriors, who were skilled riders and also much larger in stature. Over time, however, when the Khampas were eventually forced from the valleys by the Nepali government, they disbanded. Some fled, others migrated further south and a few married into the local village families of Phu. Since then, the remaining Khampa structures had been reclaimed by the villagers of Nar and Phu as their winter residences.[9]

Unlike the deserted Khampa settlements we had passed earlier, which were devoid of any life, there was movement in Kyang. Its terraced farming fields looked like they had been recently used for animal grazing, and a solitary pony roamed nearby. As we entered the village, an old woman hobbled by, bent over from the weight of a woven basket full of cut wood she was lugging on her back, while a wood-splitter axe suspended from a strap around her neck swung from side to side. She grinned at us as she passed, revealing a wide black gap in her nearly toothless mouth. Most of the other villagers we saw seemed to take little notice of us. They moved about like silent ghosts, appearing for a brief moment before disappearing among the houses as they quietly went about their business.

It was noticeably colder here. The earth was still partially frozen from the night, and a light snow began to fall as we pitched our tents. We decided to spend two days in Kyang, partly because the team needed to acclimate to the altitude, and partly because I wanted to see if Chantal's condition would improve.

After taking a quick survey of the village, I returned to our camp and pulled back the zipper of our tent to find Chantal resting inside. I sat beside her for a while before saying anything. Part of me was afraid she'd decided to return, and I wasn't ready to hear that yet.

"How are you feeling?" I finally asked.

"Awful. I took two more ibuprofens." Chantal's voice was hoarse and weak.

"We've come so far. We're so close. Maybe being here is just what you need to get to the bottom of your tension and migraine attacks," I said, but I wasn't sure of my motivation for doing so. Did I truly think there was some kind of internal demons causing these attacks that would be vanquished if Chantal simply faced up to them? Or was I just pushing this idea because I so desperately wanted to continue on to our destination?

Chantal was not swayed. "My energy level is at zero. If I decide to turn around, I'm turning around. You can go on with the boys. I'll be okay."

"But you're just as much a part of this expedition as it is a part of you. You got us here. It was you who brought us together. A couple days ago Michael told me it was because of *you* and *your* enthusiasm that he signed on and fought so hard to make it happen."

Chantal looked in my eyes for a moment. "I've run dry. I realize it was my ego driving this. We're always driving at a new goal, a new mountain, a new challenge. My true self has known for the past three years that what I truly need is a few weeks in a lawn chair with a book to read, fresh air to breathe, an easy trail for some leisurely walks, a lake to swim in, and nothing else."

It was clear I wasn't going to get an answer right now, and that pressing her further would be counterproductive. I'd have to be patient. I still held back on telling the rest of the team what was going on. I didn't want to raise the alarm just yet. My only hope was that, with two days of rest, Chantal would be able to regain enough of her strength and motivation to go forward. Somehow I was convinced that if we could just get to Phu all would be okay.

The night brought with it a cold yet calming darkness. After wrapping myself in my down sleeping bag, I began to doze off as I waited for Chantal to come back to the tent. She had stepped outside before coming to bed. Visions of a green-eyed snow leopard appeared in my half-awake, half-dream state. It was nearby, it was everywhere, it was nowhere. Ever watchful, ever quiet, it moved across the land, and the land moved with it. Just before I fell into a deep slumber, I heard the whizzing of the tent door zipper as Chantal popped her head through.

"Mike, come out here and check this out." She sounded excited, like her old self, for the first time in days.

I strapped on my boots, threw on my jacket and stepped out of the tent. The snow clouds had lifted, revealing the most stunning night sky I have ever witnessed. The entire bowl of the sky was illumined with millions of stars. Constellations glowed. Venus and Mars pulsated like bright beacons, and deep purple and orange hues stood out against the black backdrop of the night. It was one of those once-in-a-lifetime sights that stays with you forever.

I called to Arek and Jason and Michael to hurry out of their tents. All three sprang out into the open, Arek with tripod and camera in hand. Together we stood gazing out at the universe, humbled and awestruck by the spectacle around us. I turned to Chantal. A faint smile had formed on her lips, and the glitter of the night sky was reflected in her eyes.

SEVEN

Our second day in Kyang was a time for exploration. Arek, Jason, Michael and I ventured off in different directions to survey the surrounding area while Chantal continued to rest at camp. Michael positioned himself on a rock bluff, overlooking the village like a gargoyle. Arek started further up the valley to the west. Jason and I hiked up the hills to the east, where we had spotted a small herd of bharal, Himalayan mountain sheep, grazing on the hillside. It was remarkable how they blended into the barren landscape like rocks. Once we were close enough, Jason lay down on the ground, pointed his zoom lens up at the animals and began voraciously snapping photos of them – reference material he would be able to use later to create his artwork.

Leaving Jason to his photography, I headed back to camp, where I ran into Arek, who ran to me to tell me of a discovery he'd made. "Mike, I found a cave. It's high on the cliff side and has a man-made wall in front of it!"

I was instantly curious. "Did you go in?"

"No, I got part of the way up, but then I chickened out. It was too hard to get to."

"Show me."

Arek and I circled around the town, and far up on the rocky crag there it was. The cave resembled a large cleft, as though a giant axe had struck the rock face, leaving a gaping vertical crack. In front of the black void, just as Arek had said, was what was left of a neatly built rock wall. This cave had obviously been used, perhaps by the people of some forgotten civilization. Arek and I decided to check it out, and we quickly scrambled up the rock face, moving in tandem.

We passed the place where Arek had turned back. I tested the rocks as we moved, slapping the holds with my hands and gingerly positioning the front edges of my boots before placing my weight on them. "The rock is decent. These are good holds." But the higher we climbed, the less stable the rock face. The holds became looser, and many of them were no more than rocks stuck in fragile clay. Some of them popped out at my touch. Our danger suddenly became real to me. A fall at this elevation would likely be fatal. Even if we somehow survived the fall, we were in the middle of the Himalaya with no medical help nearby. I craned my neck upwards toward the black hole above us. *What secrets do you hold?* I reached out with one hand, touching the rock as though I was examining a rare gemstone. It was tempting to go on, but when I looked down to the valley floor, some 50 metres below, I gave up. "Screw it, it's not worth it." We turned back and headed down, but I took note of where we were, in case we got another opportunity to gain access to this cave and its secrets.

Above us, Michael was clambering higher up the hillside, finding himself another rock to perch on overlooking the valley.

"What is he looking for up there?"

Arek chuckled. Ever the philosopher, he answered, "I don't know. But I don't think he'll find it up there. It's within him that he'll find the answers."

Later that afternoon, we all reconvened in our mess tent, a large canvas propped up by rods where we could gather for our meals. Everyone was eager to talk about their day and the conversation was animated. Chantal took part too. The good nature and lighthearted humour of the guys was rubbing off on her. The rest day had been good for her. Her appetite was back too – just in time for the custard apple pie that our cook, Chandra, had told us he was preparing for dinner. Chandra was a short man of few words with a big heart, who took immense pride in his cooking ability. And well he should, because he never ceased to amaze us with what he could pull out of a pot over a small portable stove.

As we chattered on, waiting for dinner, our conversation came to a sudden halt at the sight of a worn boot and a weathered hand poking through the flap at the base of our mess tent. This was followed by an eye peering through a small opening at the bottom of the zipper.

I opened the flap to reveal an elderly villager standing before us. His skin was leathery, his cheekbones hollow. His eyes were dark and intense, but there was something kind and gentle about them too. He wore a traditional dark-wool *chuba* that smelled of campfire and earth. He looked like he had been living out in the open for weeks. We welcomed him in and out of the cold. He was curious about our presence, and pointed with interest at Michael's Tibetan singing bowl. Michael picked up the bowl and began to play it, circling the brass rim with the wooden mallet. Listening intently, the old man nodded, while his hands moved toward the bowl, palms up, then curled back toward his forehead, as though he was using them to sweep the bowl's reverberations into himself.

We offered him some biscuits and tea, which he accepted with apparent pleasure. As he chewed the soft biscuits, I noticed he had lost most of his teeth. Only the teeth at the front of his lower jaw still remained. Years of harsh mountain conditions, and the lack of access to medical and dental care, had clearly worn him down. It occurred to me he might not be as old as I thought. After he finished the biscuits, he said a few words in his dialect, which we didn't understand, but he motioned toward his eyes, scrunching up his face as though to indicate that they hurt. His eyes looked bloodshot. Perhaps they were windburned. Michael had some antibiotic eye drops, which he applied. They seemed to relieve his pain.

I went out to find one of our Sherpa guides to help us communicate with him, and returned with Umang, who was able to translate. We learned that his name was Pasang, that he was from Phu and that he was a yak herder who had a herd of 60 yaks. So he probably had been living out in the open, just as I had suspected from his appearance. When he heard we were heading to Phu, he seemed excited that we were going to his home village, and said there were about 30 households there that readily welcomed visitors.

When Pasang said good night to us, he placed his hands at his forehead in prayer position, then tipped them forward in our direction, as though to bless us. Or that's how we interpreted it anyway. We knew so little of his way of life. But he had given us a brief glimpse into his world, which seemed to be from another age and utterly remote from our own.

As evening fell, we were shrouded in darkness. Clouds must have been obscuring the stars, because there was no brilliant display like the one we had seen the night before. I wandered near our camp in the cold and the dark, wondering how many more Himalayan night skies I would get to see. Chantal was still undecided about whether she would turn back, and if the journey ended for her, it would also end for me. I wondered about the others, too, about what they would do. I knew the three of them were eager to get to Phu, but I didn't know how they would react to breaking the team apart.

As I strolled in the dark, the silence was broken by the sounds of Michael's guitar and a song being belted out from our mess tent.

> Strange and beautiful are the stars tonight
> That dance around your head
> In your eyes I see that perfect world
> I hope that doesn't sound too weird

The music carried in every direction, down to the valley below and up to the sky beyond the Himalayan peaks that surrounded us, enveloping the entire medieval settlement in a melodic wave of pop culture. I pulled back the flaps of canvas to find Jason had hijacked Michael's guitar and was singing the lyrics to Blue Rodeo's song, "Lost Together."

> And I want all the world to know
> That your love's all I need
> All that I need

Arek, Michael and I joined in on the chorus, half-laughing from the sheer silliness of it all.

> … And if we're lost
> Then we are lost together
> Yea if we're lost
> Then we are lost together

Maybe we were all lost together. And that was okay.

Then we broke off mid-lyric, as another weathered face poked through the opening of our tent. This time it was that of an elderly woman. She had the same cracked leathery skin and chapped lips as our friend Pasang, and the same soft eyes and gentle demeanour. At first, I thought she was going to complain and tell us to quiet down, but then she simply sat with us and looked at the guitar and Jason, wordless, as though waiting for him to resume playing. Jason passed the guitar back to Michael, who handed his Tibetan singing bowl to Arek.

Arek began turning the wood baton around the prayer bowl, setting off a deep hum. Michael let the vibrations carry for a moment before slowly starting to strum out the chords of his Nepali song – the same song he had sung with the nuns on the trail. The old woman gave a smile and nod as he began to sing in Nepali. His voice was soft and melodious. She looked on in wonderment, never shifting her gaze from Michael and his guitar, like someone watching a magic show for the first time. As Michael finished, she smiled in appreciation and gave a solid "*dhanyabad,*" which is Nepali for "thank you." Then she waited patiently, clearly hoping for another song. Michael looked at us, then started strumming the chords to Leonard Cohen's song, "Hallelujah." We all chimed in, in a gentle harmonic chorus. Our head torches swept through the darkness, warm breath flowed with the lyrics, and our visitor looked on, soaking it all in. As we closed with the last chorus, her look of wonderment turned into a wholehearted smile and she uttered words in her language that we understood without understanding.

There was something magical about having the locals come to us. It was as if we were on the verge of entering another dimension, and they'd been sent as scouts to its borders to welcome us into it. At the same time, we seemed to be serving as their entrance to our world. We sat together, touched by our Himalayan friend and the musical experience we had just shared. It was as if a common chord had been struck, resonating throughout our tent and connecting us in gratitude for each other's presence.

My eyes met Chantal's. A small flame had rekindled in her eyes, colour was returning to her cheeks and that look of adventure I knew so well was beginning to resurface. We didn't speak. We didn't need to. For in that moment I knew we were going to Phu.

Above our tent, in the silence of the night, flashes of white light danced soundlessly in the darkness, some sort of electromagnetic phenomenon that seemed to me like a celebration. Himalayan fireworks.

EIGHT

We awoke to a beautiful veil of snow. It had come down heavily through the night, covering the peaks, boulders and houses in white. The cold and the snow didn't stop us from packing up our camp in record time, as we were eager to get going. After all, the village of Phu was just ahead of us now, only a few hours away. It was good to see everyone so energized. Even Chantal had regained some of her strength. We set out at a brisk pace, circling around the north side of Kyang and passing beneath the mysterious cave Arek and I had attempted to enter. The sight of the ominous hole high up in the cliff side piqued my curiosity again, but the cave would have to wait.

Soon the massive walls of rock closed in around us, and our trail became a thin footpath carved into the sheer wall of the cliff. A couple feet to the left it dropped down to the Phu River, which rushed its way along the basin of the twisting canyon below. Towering, 6000–7000-metre-high mountains encircled us as we slowed our steps, hugging tight to the ever-narrower promontory, so small amid the vastness that we were like ants. A dramatic new perspective appeared around every bend, and each new perspective intensified our expectations of what was to come. Several bharal, the only other living beings we saw, peered curiously down at us as they stood perched on vertical terrain. If ever one could imagine an entrance into a lost valley, this surely would be it.

The cliffside trail eventually dropped back down to the valley bottom, hugging the glacier-fed Phu River. As we snaked along the riverbank, making our way north, we reached a gigantic, free-standing rock pillar that split the river. To its right, high above us at the top of the cliff, I could make out a stone gate adorned with three long prayer flags flapping forcefully in the wind. We were almost there.

Ascending the gravel switchbacks, we zigzagged our way up until we gained the ridge, and then we stood, at last, before the gates of Phu. They stopped me in my tracks. Two thick columns of neatly stacked rocks made up the pillars of the gate. The main surfaces of the pillars were dyed white, their borders deep red and the base charcoal black. Topping the pillars were aged, nearly fossilized wood beams. The beams, which appeared as hard as the stones that made up the gate, supported three small chortens, also in black, red and white, each crowned by the colourful prayer flags we'd seen from below. The centre beam of the gate's archway was inscribed with strange characters that had been carved into the wood. According to our guides – none of whom could read them – the writing was neither Tibetan nor Nepali.

The gate's hefty wooden door, reinforced with interlocking vertical wood beams and thick enough to keep intruders out, was propped open, as though to welcome us. But to what? Something about the energy here felt different than anything I'd ever felt before. It was as if the gate possessed some sort of magic, like it was a doorway into another realm.

Arek had told me about the *beyul* – sacred, hidden valleys of the Himalaya that have been sheathed in secrecy for hundreds of years. According to Tibetan Buddhism, in entering a beyul you enter a place of multiple dimensions where the physical and spiritual worlds coalesce. Believed to have been founded as places of refuge by Padmasambhava, the eighth-century Buddhist master who introduced Buddhism to Tibet, there are said to be 108 of them. About them, the Dalai Lama has said, "From a Buddhist perspective [these] sacred environments...are not places to escape the world, but to enter it more deeply... Such places often have a power that we cannot easily describe or explain.... [They] can encourage us to expand our vision not only of ourselves, but of reality itself."[10]

Keeping all this in mind, I approached the gates slowly and purposefully, listening to the crunch of the gravel underfoot. For a moment, I stood beneath the archway, feeling the sensation of being at a threshold between two worlds. And then I passed through to the other side. It was as though I had walked through an invisible force field. I became aware at once I was no longer in the world I knew. Something had shifted – in light, in colour, in sound, in feeling, in reality. Chantal came through the gates experiencing the same sensation. She gazed around at her new surroundings with a look of both joy and bewilderment, overwhelmed.

"Mike, yesterday I was in a pit of despair. I had the lowest of lows. Today, I'm having the highest high of my life."

Before us were several chortens and an intricately carved mani wall with stones dyed the same red, white and black as the gate. Brushing her hand over the mani wall, Chantal said, "I feel like the healing has only just begun."

When Arek entered, I could see he was holding back tears. "I don't deserve to be here."

We descended the ridge into the valley, passing abandoned ruins, towers from a forgotten age. Dawa believed the Tibetan warriors had built them as protection many centuries ago, in the days when warlords had competed for these lands. Circling the towers, we felt as though we were walking in the footsteps of those from an ancient civilization, their memories faded from the world, their tales lost in time.

As we walked, we saw three great red chortens and another mani wall, this one much larger, sprawled out by the river like a giant snake. When we got closer to it, we could see it looked much older than anything else we had seen on our journey. It was made up of hundreds of flat stones, each carved over and over again with the words, "om mani padme hum." Dawa placed his hand on a stone, touching the etched surface reverently as though he had connected with some unknown force. "Six sounds. Om. Ma. Ni. Pad. Me. Hum."

I searched Dawa's face. Again I asked him, "What does it mean?"

Though he hadn't answered me when I had asked him before, this time, after a long hesitation, choosing his words very carefully, he did: "Six sounds. Six places. One sound for each place."

"What are these places? Why is there a sound for each place?"

"There is place for different beings. Place for gods, place for demigods, place for humans, place for animals, place for ghosts and place for those full of anger. All places have suffering, but in each place suffering is different. The sounds bless those who suffer."

"Guys! We're up here!" Michael called down from a rise in the trail ahead.

As we rushed forward, rounding the bend, we stopped to catch our breath and take in the astonishing sight before us. We had arrived at the lost village of Phu. It was a cliffside fortress – an otherworldly place from a forgotten era, a medieval city of stone and earth, carved by hand and shaped by its harsh surroundings. Stone huts were anchored into the rock and layered upon each other up the mountainside. The people of Phu were living much as they had lived for hundreds of years.

I had heard about such places in poems and folktales but never dreamed I'd see one anywhere except in my imagination. Yet Phu was right here, in plain sight, and we were about to enter it. The buildings were stark and barren, all in tones of grey, with no sign of any kind of vegetation, as if the enormous mountains barricading the village had squeezed the very life out of it. But signs of the vital spirit of the place could be seen in the bright colours of the prayer flags flapping atop the houses, and the brilliant flashes of colour on the clothes of people we caught occasional glimpses of, which stood out vividly against the greys of the background.

Though we were not the first visitors from a foreign place to have come through their gates, there had been few enough of us that we were still a novelty. Bronze-faced women stared at us from the terraces above; the Elders studied us with their dark, serious eyes, while small children dressed in red and brown chubas lingered nearby, curious about their new visitors. One elderly woman, who was crouched over a large stone bowl washing clothes, stopped her work to acknowledge us. We did not wave to each other or make any gesture of greeting but simply looked upon each other with respect. Her face seemed to me to radiate a kindness and compassion unlike any I had seen before. She entranced me. Like the villagers we had encountered in Kyang, everyone wore thick clothes made of sheep wool, and the women had hefty stones of coral and turquoise around their necks.

We pitched our tents in one of the planting fields outside the village and regrouped in our mess tent. Sitting at the table, which one of the kitchen boys had set up for us, none of us could get many words out. We were all overwhelmed by emotion. Michael was completely still, frozen in space. His eyes were fixed, staring into nothingness as though a spell had been cast on him. He appeared to be quietly crying. Jason, too, seemed dumbstruck, his eyes tearing up beneath the large brim of his cowboy hat.

"Unbelievable," was all the Polish professor could muster.

Chantal gazed at the ground. "I can't imagine I wanted to turn back after Kyang. I was so close to it. I thought Kyang was going to be it; that I'd seen it all. And then this."

I seemed torn between breaking down into tears and doing cartwheels of joy – or both. Both reactions seemed to emanate from the same place within me, a place of reverence for all living things. The blood was coursing through my veins with such a force of energy that I could feel the vibrations under my very skin. I had waited all my life to be here, but nothing could have prepared me for the experience of being here now, as though I was standing in exactly the place I was always meant to be. I was overcome with gratitude for this moment.

And yet it wasn't long before my attention turned to the gigantic peaks that surrounded us. They were right there, right in my face. Nowhere could I look without seeing them. They called to me. They taunted me. I could think of nothing else. While the others left the mess tent – Chantal and Arek to their tents for a rest, Michael and Jason off on their own pursuits – I stayed behind to plan my next move. With my maps spread out over the entire surface of the table, I pored over them like a madman, tracking the peaks and contours of every mountain in the vicinity. There were so many of them. So many mountains, unnamed. Unclimbed. I became lost to everything and everyone around me. I was possessed by a mountain fever so strong it seized my mind, body and spirit like never before. Climbing was the only thing that mattered.

Ngawang and IC, my two Nepali climbing companions, caught the madness as well, and together we huddled around the maps like children, trying to figure out how to find our way to the pyramid mountain. We hadn't been even an hour in Phu, this magical place for which I felt such depths of emotion, yet already I was planning to leave the next day in order to go on an early-morning reconnaissance. And if we found the mountain, and conditions seemed auspicious for an ascent, then we would split off from the group and rejoin them later – perhaps in Nar, our next destination, or, if there wasn't time for that, back in Kathmandu.

I wasn't sure how Chantal would react when I told her my plan later that day, but she saw the fire in my eyes. "You have two of the best climbing Sherpas with you – go climb your mountain, Mike."

That settled it. Tomorrow we would begin our search for my mountain. From the maps I had identified an unnamed peak about 12 kilometres up an adjacent valley to the northeast, and another line of peaks about 12 kilometres further up the valley directly north. The terrain looked a little gentler to the northeast, so I decided we would start there. I didn't know where the pyramid mountain lay, but if there was one thing I was absolutely certain of, it was that I would find it.

NINE

"Maike, we will soon be in Tibet!"

IC, Ngawang and I stood at the edge of the precipice, overlooking an enormous canyon filled with glaciated ice that stretched on for several kilometres. Opposite to us on the other side of the canyon was a great mountain. Its base disappeared into a chaos of gaping crevasses. IC was concerned we would soon walk into Tibet, which would be trespassing. However, according to my map, the mountain guarded the border of Tibet like a sentinel, and the glacier acted as a moat of ice and rock, circling the peak and blocking our passage east. Tibet lay beyond the mountain, less than two kilometres from us, but inaccessible from here.

In our search for the pyramid mountain, my Nepali companions and I had travelled 12 kilometres up a remote valley to the northeast, ascending to 5030 metres, and now, having come to the edge of that massive chasm, we could go no further. We had left camp in early morning darkness and moved across the barren, high-altitude desert like ghosts. Mostly we travelled in silence, broken only by the sound of mountain winds and the cracking of glacial ice echoing up the valleys. We used the gorges to gain our ground, scampering over boulder fields and countless glacier runoffs as we ascended mountainsides of shale and snow. We passed crumbling stone chortens marking trails long forgotten, and the ruins of shelters whose inhabitants had long since vanished. We'd watched a large herd of bharal sweep down the hillside before us like a grey tidal wave, their hooves delicately brushing over the ground as though they were part of the earth. Everything moved to a different beat out here, and, like the remnants of the primordial structures we passed, it felt as though we, too, were suspended in time, with the rest of the world oblivious to our existence.

It had been an extraordinary day, but the pyramid mountain had eluded us at every step, and now our reconnaissance to the east had come to an end. The only thing left to do was to return to our camp, without having achieved our goal – or so we thought. As we made our way back to Phu, our attention abruptly shifted to the north. What came into sight at that moment stopped my breath and stole a beat from my heart. We'd missed her that morning because we'd passed her in the pre-dawn dark. But now, in full daylight, she rose from the stony earth like a gleaming white pyramid. Her sheer faces, so elegant they appeared to have been sculpted, cut straight down thousands of metres to the valley bottom. Snow and ice gilded her in a fine white veil until her slopes became so steep that nothing could stick to them, and the whiteness gave way to the black rock beneath. Her southern ridgeline, windswept and corniced, zigzagged its way to the summit like a holy passage, beckoning us to climb it. We had found our mountain, and she was even more glorious than I could have dreamed.

Ngawang, IC and I made it back to Phu as quickly as we could. It had been a very long day, 12 hours since we'd left camp, but we felt we had no time to waste. With eyes alight and our maps scattered all over the table in the mess tent, we erupted in a flurry of excitement and activity, conjuring up a new plan. I attempted to call in for permits with our satellite phone, but without knowing the name of the mountain, let alone if it even had a name, it was virtually impossible to obtain papers for it. But that didn't dissuade the two Nepali climbers. We agreed to head out for the mountain the next day in order to get a closer look, and to see what exactly we were dealing with. We'd worry about the paperwork later.

Once again I packed my bags for a reconnaissance mission, and once again, the following morning, I set out pre-dawn with Ngawang and IC, blasting up the valley with strength I didn't know I had. We wound our way up the hillsides, this time following the river northward. Apart from a few loose rocks dislodged by a herd of bharal that nearly took us out, the path was good. According to my altimeter, we had ascended to over 5000 metres by the time we crossed over into the adjacent valley.

As we descended, IC stopped in his tracks and dropped to one knee to inspect the muddy ground next to a mountain stream where the earth was still soft. He had spotted the fresh tracks of a snow leopard. I'd encountered many animals in the mountains before, but never had I come this close to a snow leopard. I knelt next to IC, gently feeling the earth, tracing the cat's print with my finger. Somehow I could feel the presence of this creature within me. We had touched the same soil, and the same mountains had summoned us both here. I searched the hillsides above us with my eyes, looking for the white ghost and wondering whether it was watching us now – although I knew seeing a snow leopard out here was virtually impossible. As I scanned the hills, soft snow began to fall, delivered by an icy wind. My gaze turned to the sky. Dark clouds were shrouding the mountain peaks, blocking our view of the horizon. We kept moving forward. But the higher we ascended, the more menacing the clouds became, the fiercer the winds and the thicker the snow. Bit by bit our visibility diminished until we could barely see each other through the gusts of snow whirling around us in white circles.

We stumbled our way into a long-abandoned settlement built of stone. Its ruins looked ancient – hundreds, perhaps thousands, of years old. It appeared as though it had once been a great village. But whoever had lived here had departed a long time ago. Many of the buildings were reduced to single walls. As the grey clouds enveloped us, and the winds whipped the snow into an ever more violent maelstrom, we hurried into one of the old stone ruins to take shelter. It was one of the few structures that still had a roof, yet the wood beams supporting the rocks on the roof were cracked and caving in. The whole thing looked as though it would collapse on us. As the blizzard grew even more ferocious, we realized we couldn't stay there. We picked up our packs and set off once again.

The snow whipped at my face and sunglasses as I attempted to survey our surroundings. Above us were the remnants of an old shrine, and above the shrine, high up in the cliffs, I could just barely make out several caves with partially barricaded walls near their entrances. Behind the walls, the ominous black holes disappeared into the rock face.

The caves, the snow leopard, our mountain, this village: so much was shrouded in mystery. My eyes caught sight of a stone lying on the ground, etched with a figure that resembled a person. The figure's head was turned to the left, its eyes glaring, and its mouth open wide with tongue extended as if to ward off evil. Its right hand was turned outward, palm up and open, from which several round objects seemed to be dropping to the ground. *What on earth happened to these people?*

I looked at IC and Ngawang. "We gotta get out of here."

TEN

Approaching Phu, we saw four Himalayan griffons scavenging the rock bluffs above the village. Their wingspan was much greater than any other bird I had seen. I'd heard of the Tibetan Buddhist custom of sky burials, in which bodies of the deceased are cut apart and their remains spread over slabs of rock for scavengers to feast on. Tibetan Buddhists believe that once the spirit leaves the body, it is but an empty vessel and should be given back to the elements.[11] Part of me was repelled by the thought of this custom, but to another part of me it made perfect sense. So much about the way of life of these people was foreign to me. Yet so much felt strangely familiar, even right. There was something in their faces, their eyes, something I couldn't really grasp, that made me feel at home with them.

By the time Ngawang, IC and I marched back into Phu, what had been a blizzard a thousand metres higher up had subsided into a calm, steady snowfall. I found our mess tent empty. The rest of the crew must have still been out exploring the village and its surroundings.

I dropped into a chair. My legs welcomed the rest after two long gruelling days of reconnaissance. For the first time on our trip I felt cold and tired. A barrage of thoughts ran through my head. I had to figure out my next move. Was I going to be able to climb that mountain or not? The weather showed no signs of letting up. And it didn't help that I had just received word that one of the mules carrying our climbing gear was lost. On top of it all, we couldn't get climbing permits for our mountain. Even though my Nepali companions were willing to climb without a permit, I wasn't comfortable putting their livelihoods at risk. Our time was running out. I was so close to reaching my dream, yet with each passing minute I could feel it slipping through my fingers. I thought about the snow leopard. I could still feel its presence. It was out there by itself, somewhere in the snowstorm. So near, yet so elusive. Fifteen years it had taken me to come this far. And for what? To be thwarted at the very foot of the mountain I had waited so long to climb?

Just then Chantal emerged through the flaps of the tent and was pleasantly surprised to find I had returned – until she saw the look on my face and listened to me vent about how frustrated I was. She knew what the pyramid mountain meant to me, knew what a blow it would be to give up on it.

"Perhaps you could get a permit for a different mountain?" she suggested. Whatever I wanted to do, she said, it was ultimately my decision to make, and she would support me however she could.

We talked about my options, but there was no reasoning it through. I felt stuck. The temperature kept dropping, so we returned to our tent to warm up in our down mummy bags. Tossing and turning, I knew I wasn't going to be able to nap. Every time I closed my eyes, I saw the mountain. I had to move. I threw on my down jacket, tuque, and boots and left the tent.

I began walking. I didn't know to where. It didn't matter. Gloomy clouds sank heavy over the village as soft snow accumulated on my jacket and hood. Except for the sound of distant goat cries, the village was quiet. I passed under the watchful eyes of a Buddha painted on a village shrine. I passed the outer wall surrounding the village houses, where human feces lined the trail. I passed a small creek running beside the village. It was filled with garbage – old clothes, the rotting sole of a shoe, dozens of tin cans and Coke bottles and plastic wrappers. Still I wandered, spending so long treading through the mud and animal dung that filled the narrow pathways in and around Phu that the bottoms of my boots were coated in several centimetres of the wet muck.

Only one other lone figure was out. From a distance it was hard to tell who it was, but it appeared to be an old woman, whose face was obscured by the thick wool cloak she'd wrapped around herself. She stood atop the terrace outside her home, looking out over the valley. As though sensing my presence down below, the old woman turned toward me. I narrowed my eyes, trying to get a clearer view of her through the snowfall. I couldn't make out her face, but I could feel her eyes on me. For a moment, I felt as though she was speaking to me through her eyes. Somehow she reminded me of the etching on the stone I'd found outside the abandoned settlement, and I wondered if she was trying to warn me. But warn me of what? I did not know. The old woman slowly retreated from her terrace and disappeared inside.

I kept wandering until eventually I returned to our mess tent to find Michael sitting there by himself. With his wool tuque, fingerless gloves and grey city jacket, he looked as though he was about to busk on a busy downtown street in Vancouver. After having been shocked into a state of awe so profound he could barely speak when we first arrived in Phu, Michael had quickly adapted and now seemed entirely at home. A song was never far from his lips, and his music had helped him make friends among the villagers. They were particularly intrigued by the fact that he travelled with a Tibetan singing bowl, and had even composed a song in Nepali. I was intrigued at his ability to be able to find such pleasure and contentment in what he did, while I was always so driven to keep moving; to climb the next mountain, to find another peak.

I spoke to him about the events of our two days of reconnaissance, which looked as though they were going to come to nothing in the end. Although Michael, as well as Arek and Jason, knew the pyramid mountain was one of my objectives in going to the Nar Phu valley, and were aware I was planning to take a couple of the guides and split off from the team for a few days or even longer in order to climb it, they hadn't really known how obsessed I was. But now I told Michael about the desolation I felt at the possibility of not being able to fulfill my long-held dream. About how climbing was an essential part of me, and that without it I was lost. Circumstances seemed to be working against me, but some part of me was still hoping to rescue my climb. I was torn, not knowing whether to keep pushing, as I'd always done, or to trust the signs that seemed to be telling me not to. How would I feel if I walked away from the mountain now, when I had come so close? Michael remained mostly silent as I continued the "Jekyll and Hyde" conversation with myself.

"What does this journey mean to you?" he finally asked.

It was a good question. It was as though everything within me felt I should be climbing the mountain. Yet everything around me was pulling me away from it. Pulling me to where, I did not know. I thought about the old woman we had encountered after branching off the Annapurna Circuit, the one who seemed to feel such a connection to Chantal. About Sonam Dorje, the young man who had welcomed us so warmly into the longhouse at Koto. About the two villagers we had met in Kyang–Pasang, who had gestured such a kind blessing toward us, and the old woman who listened to Michael's music with such intensity. About the people we'd met at the tea house in Meta and how hospitable they had been. About the nuns who had joined us on the trail so companionably, and Nishta, the young woman who had joined Michael in his song. Even the little girls who had swarmed "Shanti" in Bhulbhule had seemed to act from such a deep wellspring of joy and laughter. It was as though the hardships of their lives had left them untouched. I thought about every other villager we had encountered up here and along the trail, people in whom I sensed some kind of generosity of spirit that spoke to me, tugged at my heart. What was this deep familial connection I felt to them? Why did I feel their eyes were like a mirror into my very soul? They seemed to have something I had lost, or perhaps had never possessed.

I had to make a choice. I knew that if I walked away from my dream I would have to live with the disappointment for a long time. Yet it seemed as though my fate was in the hands of something greater than my own will. And so I chose to trust in that. I would stay with our team in Phu. The mountain was for someone else to climb.

ELEVEN

Once I made my decision, it felt good to be back in the company of my friends. I realized how little time we had spent together once we got to Phu, and how little I had participated in their explorations of the village.

Although the next day dawned dark and cloudy, and the snowfall continued, I decided to wander around and see some more of Phu. During my walk, I came across an abandoned stone building, which appeared to be the shell of what had once been a school. Three wooden benches sat empty in the classroom. A blackboard lay on the ground with the faded chalk marks of Nepal's national flag, as though class had stopped one day and never resumed. Not for the first time I had to wonder what would become of the children of these remote Himalayan villages who had little chance of an education. That was why Sonam Dorje's parents had spent everything they had to send him to school.

I passed an old outhouse, perhaps something the government had built but long ago ceased to maintain. It was overflowing with human feces, and more feces were piled around it. I kept circling within the labyrinth of the village, meandering higher and higher, until I found myself at the very top. Crowning Phu was a large structure that resembled a fortress. It was the most elaborately crafted building in the whole village, but it had fallen into ruins. I stood there, gazing out from the fortress to the medieval stone houses below, which seemed to be hanging on for life.

"Harsh" didn't even begin to scratch the surface of what life was like out here. The people of Phu had made their home in the high Himalaya, one of the most inhospitable places on Earth. Nothing came easy for them. Every day was a new fight to survive. Only those with the endurance and tenacity to match the unforgiving elements would endure. And sometimes even that wasn't enough. My thoughts turned to the ancient ruins where we had taken shelter during the blizzard. Were the people of Phu destined to die out or disappear? If so, this would mean the end of a way of life that had gone on for hundreds, perhaps even thousands, of years. What would be lost in the event of their extinction? Would the world be any the poorer for their absence? These were sobering thoughts, and I wondered what could be done to ensure that life would continue in these remote Himalayan villages. In light of the possible disappearance of an entire people and their culture, the feelings of disappointment I had felt over my foiled mountain-climbing plan seemed trivial.

I stood under the sunless sky watching the cloud masses tumble upon each other, searching the horizon for a break in the clouds, even a sliver of blue. But it did not come, and the grey of the morning matched my mood as I wondered what fate might have in store for this village.

The next day, through drifts of snow that blurred my vision, I could just barely make out a figure approaching our camp from across the field. He walked alone, but his stride quickened as he caught sight of me.

"Namaste-eeee!" the familiar voice echoed. It was Sonam Dorje, the young man we had met in Koto, whom I had just been thinking about. He had made it to Phu a couple days before we did, and after seven years of studying Tibetan Buddhism in India had finally reunited with his parents. He described his homecoming and how happy he had been to see his family again. Despite his worries, he had instantly recognized his mother and father. They had recognized him too, even though he had obviously changed a lot, having left when he was only 14 and returned as an adult.

After inquiring about our time in Phu, Sonam suggested that he take us to the Tashi Lhakhang gompa, as he had something he wanted to show us there. Tashi Lhakhang was the monastery Dawa had mentioned to me earlier, when he advised me to ask the lama stationed there about the meaning of "om mani padme hum," so I was eager to go.

I gathered our team and together we followed our young friend up the steep switchbacked trail. The higher we ascended, the more rocks we saw with the Tibetan mantra "om mani padme hum" carved on them, until there were hundreds of the smooth etched stones covering the hillside. Amid them, 17 colourful chortens lined the trail, their vertical prayer flags flapping in the wind. It wasn't long before we reached the top of the hill, and with it an unobstructed vista over the Lost Valley to the south. Towering, snow-capped mountains squeezed the valley from either side, pushing the Phu River into a narrow gorge. Rocky hillsides, stark and barren, rose from the valley floor before giving way to the icy giants. And there below us, clinging to the edges of a solitary rock mound, was the tiny village of Phu. Its buildings, decrepit and crumbling, clustered tightly together as though the village was making a last stand, refusing to yield to the powerful forces of nature that encircled it.

I shifted my gaze to Sonam. He looked downcast, worried.

"This, my village. It is disappearing."

His words were an uncanny echo of my thoughts of the previous day, and I wondered what Sonam had in mind. "Why do you say that?" I asked.

"There is no health care here. No education. No electricity. And the nearest road is five-day trek away."

"But it has survived for hundreds of years."

"Yes, but things are changing. Those who are sick, or old, they just die in their home. Children run around, without school. Anyone who has enough money will leave this village."

"Is it not good for people to leave to get educated, if there is no school here? That's what you did."

"Yes, but not many come back. Some come back, but their minds already changed. In Phu we have own culture. Our own language. When they return, it's too late. They are different."

"They lose their culture?"

"Yes, this I am thinking. If this problem keeps happening, our culture will be lost." He gazed into the distance as he surveyed his village. "My village, gone forever."

"Could you not lead the change for your people?" Chantal asked. "Could you bring a health post and education into Phu?"

"This is my dream. But very expensive. And many villagers do not listen to me since they have no education, and because I am young."

As we wandered the monastery grounds, Sonam spotted a *dungchen*, a ceremonial Tibetan horn, over two metres in length, which he found resting upright outside the temple's main entrance. This was the first instrument we had seen since entering the Lost Valley, and it was remarkable-looking, forged of bronze and reinforced with elaborately decorated brass clasps. Sonam weighed it in his hands before placing his lips to its mouthpiece. With his cheeks puffed, he blew into the horn, releasing a deep bellow that reverberated over the valley in a single transcendent tone, as though the mountains themselves had spoken. It was a divine sound that carried with it the memory of a time long passed.

We tried to enter the monastery to search for the lama, but the doors were locked, and he was nowhere to be found. I was beginning to think my perennial question about the meaning of "om mani padme hum" would go unanswered. So I asked Sonam instead. The young man thought about it as he paced slowly alongside one of the mani walls, turning its rickety prayer wheels. "It is blessing. All life has suffering. But to live is to suffer. So we bless life, we bless death, we bless sickness and health, we bless happiness and sadness. We say om mani padme hum to bless all suffering borne by all beings, as the suffering is our karma. And our karma is our life."

I took comfort in Sonam's words. They moved me. I had never heard someone speak of suffering in such a way. If my karma was indeed my life, then where was this flow of events leading me? Before us, the Phu River descended through the valley, snaking its way around the boulders. It flowed without thought or knowledge of its destination; unaware of what lay beyond the next bend, and the bend after that. Yet it flowed where it must, meeting the Nar River and becoming one with it, before hurtling down yet another valley. If this was the way of the river, perhaps this was also the way of life.

With that thought, it was time to leave. But just then Arek called us over. He had found a single, baby-sized footprint in a rock near the monastery. It has been said that this is the symbol Padmasambhava used to demarcate the beyul valleys. Whether this is true or not, I certainly did believe we had found a sacred place.

Over the next three days in the Lost Valley, I became absorbed in the village life of Phu. The deeper I immersed myself, the more I lost track of time, which seemed to flow – like the rivers I'd watched from the monastery – without any apparent beginning or end. I no longer looked at my watch; instead, I measured the hour by the movements of the people and events around me.

Each day began with the cries of babies and the ear-piercingly loud voices of women calling to each other from their rooftops, breaking the pre-dawn stillness. Though to us these voices sounded urgent, dramatic, according to Dawa the women were simply making plans for the day ahead, discussing who was headed for which fields at what time, and catching up on gossip.

An hour or so later, we'd see some of the women making their way out of town, herding the goats that lived in shelters beneath their homes when they weren't grazing in the fields. Other women began the steep climb to a plateau high above the village to plant barley and potatoes. Still other women, both young and old, as well as a few old men, congregated in the centre of the village where there was a small temple. There they gathered to spin yak wool. Small children played nearby, usually a simple game of kick the can, when they weren't watching their parents and grandparents spin the wool.

But if Michael was around, which he often was, they flocked around him. Children and adults alike were always fascinated with Michael's music and guitar. Communicating through the language of his music, he never failed to captivate an audience. Though the locals loved listening to Michael, they didn't seem to have much music themselves. Except for the dungchen we'd seen at the monastery, we never saw a musical instrument of any kind. Michael did hear the villagers singing occasional folk songs, which Dawa told him were work songs and songs about the mountains – but that was about it for music. So far as we could tell, no one in the village even owned a radio, nor would there have been any reception even if they did.

During the day, Arek and Jason would venture into the village or nearby hills to observe the locals and their culture. Arek spent hours every day photographing the villagers as they went about their business, as well as their homes and their animals and shrines. Jason, sketchbook and pencils in hand, sought out unique architectural and cultural artifacts to sketch. On one of their excursions they went to the ruins of the fortress at the top of the hill, where Jason noticed a finely engraved slate stone carving of what appeared to be three Buddhas hanging above one of the open doorways. He carefully removed the relief and placed it on the ground. Taking three pages from his journal, he gently traced over every inch of the engravings with a soft pencil, creating three embossed rubbings. He feared the images he created might one day be all that was left of this ancient slate, for it was exposed to the elements and hung from a wooden peg that could easily rot away in the harsh conditions and allow the tablet to drop to the ground and shatter into pieces. He could not preserve the tablet itself – which he felt belonged in a museum – but at least he could capture its images and prevent them from being permanently lost.

Chantal and I spent much of our time wandering the village and the areas around it, sometimes with Sonam. We learned that the small government school I'd seen on an earlier walk had indeed been abandoned, as no teacher was willing to accept the meagre government salary to tolerate the harsh conditions and remoteness of Phu. We also learned there was no form of health care in the village, no toilets and the only electricity came from small solar panels that the government had installed years ago, although most of the panels were broken now and not functioning.

Sonam told us the villagers welcomed tourism from trekkers like us, because the rupees we paid as our "tenting tax" would go directly to the village. Yet while they were open to tourists because of the economic benefits, many minds remained closed; most of the village Elders were largely stuck in their ways. They were reluctant to listen to suggestions of progress from younger people like Sonam, even the few who were educated. For Sonam, who was very aware that a balance had to be maintained between tradition and progress, this was very frustrating. As he had expressed earlier, he feared the village way of life would die out entirely if the villagers made no concessions to modernization.

In the evening, our group usually spent time with the locals in their homes, sharing meals and each other's company. On one such evening, we were invited to a large social gathering. When we arrived there were ten women crouched around the dung-fuelled stove. The stove served as a source of heat, as well as the principal source for cooking. A narrow stove-pipe carried some of the smoke – but not nearly all of it – through a hole in the roof. The dwelling and everything in it reeked of smoke and soot. Gradually, more women and a few men arrived, some with their children, packing themselves so tightly into the small room that there was almost no space to move. The women began to prepare the small Tibetan dumplings filled with mashed potato called *momos*, while the men, grime-stained and covered in dirt, caught up on the events of their day in the mountains. Some of the children helped out with the making of the momos, while the very young sat quietly, taking in the whole spectacle.

As with most of these encounters, we didn't communicate with each other in words since we had no shared language. And even Dawa, who was with us that night as he often was, could translate only part of what was being said because the dialect in Phu was so different from Nepali. But it didn't matter. We communicated through body language, and the language of the eyes, and always felt welcomed.

It wasn't long after the tiny dumplings were placed in a steaming pot over the stove that they were ready to eat and served. The momos were passed around the room, followed by a large bottle of Sprite, from which each person poured a sip into his or her mouth without ever touching the bottle's rim to their lips.

Eventually, a young fiery woman named Sangita piped up. She had been observing us over the course of the evening. She actually knew many English words, and requested, or almost demanded in a rather imperious tone of voice, that Michael play her a song – as though she was skeptical about his ability to produce any sort of music at all. The room hushed and all eyes turned to Michael. Smiling to himself, perhaps with a bit of smugness, he broke into his Nepali song. The room, even the children, fell silent, and we watched as Sangita's expression softened and her eyes locked on Michael, seemingly unable to turn away. As Michael finished the last verse, and the vibrations of his guitar strings began to fade, the room remained still, until Sangita broke the silence with a simple "I love you." I'm not sure if everyone understood what she said – maybe even Sangita herself didn't quite understand – but a tidal wave of laughter erupted throughout the room.

As the night progressed, so too did the local customs, which meant that *raksi*, an alcoholic beverage made from millet and distilled in the locals' homes, was introduced into the mix. The women mostly stayed away from the drink, but the men, including Dawa, seemed to enjoy it immensely. The clear liquid burned my throat as it went down and left a gasoline-like aftertaste in my mouth. One sip of raksi was enough for me, customary seconds or not. After a glass or two, Dawa himself broke into a deep, melodious Sherpa song from his homeland, serenading us with songs of strawberries, youthful love and plentiful crops.

Arek snapped photos as the events unfolded, and the villagers showed great interest in his photography – particularly in studying all the dials and buttons on his SLR camera and its digital screen. There was not a single camera in Phu, and any of the locals who somehow managed to obtain a photograph of a family member would proudly display it on the mantel of their home. Such photos, however, were rare, and the few we saw were weathered and faded.

A few days before, Arek had mused, "I come into a place like this and *take* photos. But what do I give?" Seeing how much the villagers cherished the few family photos they had, Arek decided he would do a professional photo shoot for them. He had told Dawa he would like to do this, but Dawa thought it would be too much of a challenge to gather a large group for a shoot. Now, however, with around 20 of Phu's villagers all in one room, it seemed like the opportune time. And Dawa knew it. Smiling his contagious smile, the Sherpa stood up and announced to the room, "Picture time!"

The lively chatter turned to whispers and muffled laughter at this announcement. Many of the women were eager to have their portraits taken but embarrassed about it, so each one was trying to encourage the others to go first, but none of them was willing. And then, amid all the banter about who would start, one of the villagers, a silent, gruff-looking man who had sat quietly in the corner for most of the evening, stood up and walked confidently before Arek. Surprised by what had just happened, Arek was still for a moment then suddenly snapped into motion, scrambling to figure out a suitable setting for the portraits and getting his camera into position. After watching the proceedings, the other men began lining up, and one by one Arek took their portraits. The men then requested a group photo, and they arranged themselves, arms clasped around each other, while Arek happily snapped away. And while the women were too shy to have their portraits taken separately, they warmed up to having their photos taken together. Stoic expressions in front of the camera turned into laughter. And for a moment the tough and hardened mountain women became soft, fun-loving free spirits.

After the last photo was snapped, Arek promised to print out the portraits and send them back after our return to Canada. We knew Mick would likely be coming back to Phu in the fall, and we would be able to send the photos along with him. The villagers were thrilled by the promise of this gift. They remarked on the fact that the few foreigners who had come through their village took many photos of them, but they themselves never got to own them or even see them.

Being with the people of Phu continued to evoke strange emotions of homecoming within me. As though I had found long-lost brothers and sisters from a previous life. Never had I experienced such open kindness from complete strangers in a land so far from my own. Such compassion. Such acceptance.

In the time remaining, I continued to spend many hours talking with Sonam Dorje, who had so much insight into the problems facing his village. In the home he shared with his parents and other family members, he would serve me butter tea (which I had finally acquired a taste for), and I would ask him endless questions about his people and their customs and culture.

Like the other houses I had been in, Sonam's was a single room, with all the activity centred on the dung- and wood-fuelled stove in the middle of the room. A colourful and elaborately carved wooden cabinet spanned one wall and contained most of their belongings – which included dishes, cooking utensils, copper and steel pots and a few cooking ingredients. In one corner of the room was a small shrine, adorned with pictures of Buddha, a photograph of the 14th Dalai Lama and a row of butter tea lights. Each item in Sonam's home had its place and was neatly displayed and well polished, as if his parents took great pride in everything they owned. After I had returned to Canada, I was looking at some of the photos I had taken in Sonam's home and I noticed that, beneath the shrine, there was a picture of a boy wrapped in wool clothes, sitting astride a horse with two full saddle bags draped over its body, as though about to go on a long journey. Next to the boy was a man who had what looked like an expression of pride on his face. I couldn't help but wonder if the boy in the photo was Sonam, and the man his father, perhaps on the day Sonam left his family, his home and his world to make his way to India, where he would study for the next seven years before finding his way home again.

During our time together, Sonam and I walked the narrow village paths as I listened to his concerns about the threat to his people's way of life. He pointed out houses that had fallen into ruin, which had once been occupied by people who had since left the village. Anyone with money, he said, was likely to leave in order to live in a community more connected to the outside world, with greater access to such amenities as health care and education. They might go to Koto, or even as far as Kathmandu. There was no doubt Sonam loved his village and his people very much, and that he valued their long-held customs and way of life. However, I began to sense a tone of disillusionment in the young man's voice. Earlier he had told me that when people came back from the outside world they had changed too much, had ceased to care for the old ways of doing things, the old values. Perhaps, during his time in Darjeeling he, too, had been influenced by his time in the modern world and was now realizing that world moved at a faster pace – and he along with it – than his village did. I wondered if he was struggling with the same questions I was – questions about what was lost and what was gained by being part of the modern world. Could Phu hold onto what made it so special if it, too, began to modernize?

On our last long walk, Sonam and I passed four elderly women sitting with their backs to a stone wall. One of the women began rattling off words in my direction, pointing at me with intensity.

"What is she saying?" I asked Sonam.

Sonam glanced sideways at me, a little embarrassed. "She is saying, that in your previous life you were one of us. In your previous life, you were my grandfather."

* * *

During the days I had immersed myself into village life, I scarcely noticed the thick clouds were lifting, allowing the sun to re-emerge and spread its warmth over the valley. Nor had I noticed how quickly the time was passing, until suddenly it was our last day in Phu. I decided to bring the team up to the ruins of the old village where Ngawang, IC and I had been caught in the snowstorm. The gigantic snow-capped mountains, which had been almost invisible that day through the blizzard, were now revealed in all their glory. At the head of the valley was none other than the pyramid mountain. Her peak shone brightly as the sun's rays reflected off the fresh snow. I looked to my friends. Chantal was wandering among the abandoned buildings, brushing the old stones with her hands as she gazed to the looming Himalaya, drawing healing energy from their magnificence. Jason was captivated by the snow leopard print, meticulously taking its measurements so he could recreate it in a drawing once he was back in Canada. Michael and Arek were simply basking in the sun, surveying the Himalayan vistas with contented grins. IC and Ngawang searched excitedly on their hands and knees for *yatze gumba*, a rare fossilized Himalayan larva that was worth more than its weight in gold.

I only had eyes for my mountain. Seeing her again in all her splendour briefly rekindled the fire inside me, and with it the ache in my stomach, which I thought I had vanquished. But the mystery of why I was leaving my dream behind still vexed me. And then I thought about what I had gained by relinquishing it – the opportunity to share a profound journey to a remarkable place with my friends and the one I love – and again I found a measure of peace with my decision.

Our expedition in the Himalaya was nearing its end. We would be making one last stop, in the neighbouring village of Nar, another place we wanted to explore, before starting on the journey back to Kathmandu, and then home. Originally, we had planned to stay only one day in Nar, but my decision not to attempt the pyramid mountain meant we would have a couple of extra days there.

Before leaving Phu, I ventured into the village to bid one last farewell to Sonam. When I found him, I could see a sadness in his eyes I had not seen before. "You will never come back here, will you." It was more of a statement than a question.

I didn't know how to answer him. In our Western world, it is common on parting to exchange meaningless pleasantries about how happy we will be to see each other again – when, in fact, we know this will not happen and do not intend to try. I couldn't bear to make a show of this kind of hypocrisy to Sonam. I cared for him deeply, and he and his parents and their community had offered us such genuine hospitality. The truth was I didn't know if I would see Sonam again, though I doubted it. By way of an answer, I took the young man's hand and held it firmly. Our eyes connected, and for a moment we understood each other. Then, cinching the hip belt of my backpack, I turned to the south and did not look back.

TWELVE

We passed beneath the gates of Phu as though we had exited through an invisible door. On one side was the energy vortex, and on the other was a world far more familiar. Although, this time there was something markedly different about it. Colours looked sharper and more vibrant than they had before, and my senses were filled with a heightened awareness of the interconnectedness of all things. A deeper level of understanding had opened, and I could somehow feel the strength of an unseen force guiding me. There was truth in the Dalai Lama's words about the beyul – I had no doubt about it. We had been visitors in a sacred refuge, and my vision of reality, and of myself, had truly expanded.

We followed the Phu River southward, circling around the old Khampa settlements we had passed on the way up. Chantal looked around in wonder. Now that she had regained her strength, she registered her surroundings as though she was seeing these places for the first time – places she had been in too much distress to notice on our way up.

Once again, the valley began to close in around us as we hugged the narrow winding route along the cliff side. Rounding each bend, I stretched my neck to catch final glimpses of the towering peaks before they disappeared from view. I knew I had to trust in the force pulling me down the valley and away from them.

We marched onward, descending with each step, until the canyon began to widen and I knew the settlement of Kyang was near and, with it, the Kyang cave Arek and I had attempted to access. The closer we came to the cave, the more my curiosity grew, until I stood beneath the cave, looking up at the ominous black hole high in the cliff side. There was a pent-up energy and restlessness inside me, which I attributed to having walked away from my dream, and I felt I had to see what was in that cave. I threw my pack to the ground and began to scale the rock face. I didn't know what I was looking for, but I would not rest until I entered that void.

My Sherpa companions, Umang and Ngawang, climbed with me, and together the three of us scrambled up the rocky ledges as the others looked on from below. The higher we climbed, the more I could feel the open air under my feet. The rock began to deteriorate, forcing me to slow my movements. I glanced down about 30 metres to the bottom of the valley. My palms were getting sweaty. Just as I remembered from my first attempt, the rock had turned loose and crumbly, and some of the holds were no more than stones wedged into hard clay. One rock dislodged at my touch, bouncing down to the base of the cliff. *Don't think, just move*, I told myself. The three of us kept moving in tandem, gingerly placing step after step, and feeling for hold after hold, until we stood before the gaping black hole I had gazed at from the valley floor. The cave looked more daunting up close, and I could feel a cold breeze coming from deep within the darkness in front of us. I took a breath, flicked on my head torch and entered into the abyss.

We crammed ourselves up the natural chimneys, scrambling over boulders wedged inside the narrow fissure. Fine, ash-like sand slid down the walls as we shimmied ourselves up, shelf after shelf, often jamming our bodies through openings so tight we could barely squeeze ourselves through. Bat droppings were everywhere, and it was clear no one had been in here for a very long time.

Soon we emerged into a small cavern at the back of the cave. It felt good to stand upright and on level ground again. The air was cool and dry and smelled of cold rock. As I stepped into the cavern, I could feel the ground beneath my boot give way and heard a dull crunching sound. For a moment, it felt as though I had stepped on eggshells. I shone my light on my feet and nearly gasped when my mind registered what was beneath us. In the light of my torch, empty eye sockets were staring back at me. We were standing on a pile of human bones. Hundreds of bones – arms, legs, ribs and skulls – littered the cavern floor.

"What the hell?"

Umang picked up what looked to be a large femur and then part of a spinal cord. The cavern walls sparkled behind him. The ash-like sand that lined the walls on the way in had turned into some sort of crystalized mineral. I scanned the gleaming cavern interior with my head torch as young Umang kept examining the bones, holding up a jawbone so large his entire face fit inside it. A yellow molar that looked three times the size of a regular molar was still affixed to the jaw.

The eeriness of it all was getting to me. This wasn't just a cave. It was a tomb, and it had probably been located in such an inaccessible place to keep people away – yet we had trespassed on it. I could see Ngawang was also uneasy. He remained near the exit of the cavern. I suddenly felt anxious and wanted to get out of there as fast as possible. Trying not to disturb anything more than we already had, the three of us backed away from the tomb and retraced our steps out of the cave. Exiting the darkness, and re-emerging into the light of the sun, we were glad to see Chantal and the others patiently waiting for us below.

Once we got to Kyang and asked the inhabitants about it, we discovered the cave was a mystery to them too. No one our Sherpas spoke with, not even a 70-year-old woman who seemed to be the oldest person in the village, knew anything about the bones in the cave. Curiosity sprouted like a seed within my mind as I speculated about the lives we had stumbled on. What was their story? Questions about their past – about where they had come from, who they were, what had happened to them, why they were buried there, hidden so deep inside the cliff, whether they had left any other records of their existence – kept circling around in my head.

Sonam's fear for the survival of his village began to fill my mind. I'd wondered if Phu was destined to disappear, and now I wondered about what had happened to the community whose bones I had just discovered. How long had these people lived here before vanishing? And when had they vanished? Was it the fate of such civilizations, with their thousands of years of history, to simply disappear without anyone seeming to notice or to remember them?

Sobered and somewhat shaken for the moment, we continued our way south. We walked silently, each of us processing, in our own very different ways, all we had experienced in the last week. Arek seemed spaced out; Jason, wide-eyed and curious as ever; Michael, subdued, his guitar kept in its case; Chantal, revitalized. We had been through the kind of life-altering journey that needed to be questioned. Deconstructed. Examined. As though we now had to make new sense of the way we looked at the world, and our lives within it.

My mind kept turning over the bones in the cave and the sacred ground we had stumbled upon. I couldn't help but think about the burial site – that it suggested the dead were being protected. Perhaps the cave had been sanctified as a doorway, a portal through which one passed from the end of life to the beginning of a new one.

Dawa, who by now had become so familiar with my way of thinking that he seemed like an old friend, caught up with me just then. "Maike," he began. I could always tell when he was about to say something serious. His usually cheerful expression would turn thoughtful, almost solemn, and his eyes became intense. "I have thought about it for days."

"About what?"

"I would like to give you Sherpa name. You have Sherpa blood in you."

His words caught me by surprise. I was so moved I was left speechless and could only reciprocate the depth of the Sherpa's gaze.

"Your Nepali name is Tsering Sherpa. It means 'Long Life.'"

I was deeply touched. It felt perfect, as though it was a name I already knew, perhaps from another lifetime, if the old woman who had identified me as Sonam's grandfather was correct. I nodded in acknowledgement and with gratitude. Together, the light-footed Sherpa and I continued along the trail, both of us silent, taking in the majestic views. Above us, the mighty Himalaya basked in the sunlight. Spindrift blew from the high ridges like white sand being cast into the open air.

My mind took me back to the Lost Valley. Not just to the old woman who had said I was Sonam's grandfather. But to Sonam himself, and all the other people we had befriended in Phu. To thoughts of the pyramid mountain, and thoughts of the forces pulling me away from it. To thoughts of the mysterious snow leopard. To thoughts of the bone cave and the lost civilization that had performed burials there. And, finally, to thoughts of the name Dawa had chosen for me. The way they all kept drifting in and out of my head, in some kind of holding pattern, it was as though there was some intricate force connecting them that I needed to understand. But maybe there was no meaning to them. Maybe there didn't need to be. Then again, maybe it was all part of some kind of overarching order that would one day be revealed to me. Or perhaps all that mattered was the meaning I chose to give to them, and that would be the revelation I was searching for.

Before long, a new valley opened in the distance, branching off to the west. Dawa pointed to the horizon. "That is where we go. Beyond those hills is village of Nar."

I turned my gaze to the west, toward the hills Dawa had indicated, tracing the horizon with my eyes. For the first time in many weeks, a gentle warmth brushed my face.

PART TWO

A LITTLE GIRL

THIRTEEN

The great mani wall stretched across the open plain like a castle wall – stark, monumental, awe-inspiring. The wall looked centuries old. Its stones had been laid carefully over time, each one placed by a nomad who had travelled alongside it, echoing the eternal blessing of "om mani padme hum." Its chortens stood tall, resembling a row of watchtowers lining the entrance to a kingdom – though what the wall and chortens led to was not a kingdom but the small village of Nar. Yet it was a grand entrance if ever I'd seen one – a majestic human creation worthy of the snow-capped mountains overlooking it. The 7000-metre Kang Guru Mountain dominated the eastern skyline like a white giant. To the south, the enormous Pisang Peak barricaded the horizon with serrated waves of ice-covered ridgelines. To the north and west of us were rugged brown hills and rock formations.

We'd arrived at Nar two days after leaving Phu. Our first night on the trail we'd camped at a site called Nar Phedi, which rested in the gorge of the Phu valley alongside the Nar River, where a new monastery was being built. In the morning we'd hiked back out of the canyon and, following the winding trail westward, we crested a pass, walked through the first of the Nar gates, a stone structure far more modest than the gate to Phu, and descended into the valley where the village of Nar was nestled. Unlike the north-south aspect of the Phu valley, the Nar valley had an east-west orientation, which opened it to more daylight and warmth from the sun, and made it much drier and less windy than the Phu valley.

After passing the mani wall and the second of the Nar gates, also a very modest structure, we skirted the hillside and rounded another couple of bends, and at last the village of Nar revealed itself. It was but a small cluster of buildings set amid a vast alpine basin. From afar, the brown stone structures nearly faded into the rocky bluffs. Beneath the village we could see planting fields, and beyond the fields, at the bottom of the valley, the Ghatte River. If Phu was an isolated bastion clinging to the mountain above, Nar was the gentle stroke of a brush, painted against the backdrop of the grey Himalayan plateau.

As we approached the village, we came under the shadow of Pisang Peak. Its snow-crested summit taunted me, reminding me of what I had given up. Our expedition was nearing its end and I hadn't done what I'd set out to do. Some part of me still felt like a failure for not having fulfilled my dream, and I had to struggle to remind myself to just keep trusting in the ever-unfolding flow of events.

My companions were also processing the events of the past several weeks, each in their own different ways. Jason was capturing the experience through his art, which seemed to be absorbing more and more of his energy, as he was rarely to be seen these days without his paintbrushes and sketchbook, while Arek appeared to be using the journey as a springboard into his future, a way of getting a fresh perspective on his life. Chantal gave the impression of someone who was living in a constant state of wonder, while Michael seemed haunted by both the beauty and the transience of the way of life we'd witnessed. Not long before we got to Nar, he had taken it upon himself to collect garbage and litter that was left alongside the trails. "Can you believe it," he erupted, having spotted a plastic grocery bag, "even in the middle of the Himalaya, you can't go anywhere without finding a plastic bag rustling in the bushes!" The sight of that bag had provoked him, because it suddenly represented so much more than just another piece of trash. To Michael it was a sign of how this pristine land we'd been privileged to see was being encroached upon by the modern world. He couldn't do much about that, but he could pick up a bag, so he did. Soon we were all inspired to pitch in, and by the time we arrived in Nar, around noon, we had filled an entire burlap sack with an assortment of rusted cans, plastic wrappers and pop bottles.

Once in Nar, we discovered a tea house that had rooms for travellers and decided to stay there – a welcome change from weeks of sleeping in our tents. After settling in, Arek and Jason went off to explore the village, while Michael occupied himself teaching our young Sherpa guide, Umang, to play the guitar. Chantal and I just relaxed, happy to do nothing for a while. Chantal was herself again, lighthearted and cheerful as she basked under the blue skies, which, after many days of gloomy weather, were a welcome sight. I lay in the parched dust in a small courtyard outside the tea house, scratching at the layers of Himalayan dirt that had bonded to the fabric of my pants over the weeks of trekking. As I stretched out, resting my head on a soft tuft of grass and feeling the warmth of the sun on my face, I began to drift off. Thoughts floated in a jumble through my mind, my vision blurred and I felt my body sinking into the earth around me.

Hours passed in a half-waking-, half-dream-like state, during which I lost all track of time, until Arek and Jason returned from their walk.

"How was it?" I asked, still lying down, with the rim of my ball cap still pulled over my eyes.

"The villagers here seem more accustomed to outsiders," Arek mused. "I met a boy who took an interest in my necklace. I jokingly suggested we swap, but he declined."

"Smart kid."

Like their parents, the children of Nar and Phu wore necklaces of turquoise and coral. We had discovered it was the custom for these necklaces to be passed down from generation to generation. It was one of the only valuable possessions – and undoubtedly the most valuable – that most of these children would ever own, far more valuable than the colourful string of wooden beads Arek had pieced together from a Salt Spring Island bead shop.

"And we met the school teacher."

At those words, I pulled my cap from my eyes and propelled myself upright. Kang Guru Mountain was glowing orange as the sun began to disappear behind the horizon, and I realized I'd spent the entire day in a pleasant stupor. But now I was wide awake.

"This village has a school?"

"Yeah. The teacher's not from around here, though. In fact, he pretty much said he feels like he's been banished to the end of the earth. He invited us to come by tomorrow morning."

I thought back to what Sonam told me about how far he had to travel for his own education, and how discouraged he felt about the possibility of bringing education to Phu because of the cost and the resistance of some of the villagers. I remembered the deserted schoolhouse in Phu, and the little children running around in tattered clothes, their days empty of any sense of direction until they were old enough to work in the fields – a time that would come only too soon. While their Elders would pass the traditional village knowledge down to them, their access to any education beyond that would be nonexistent, unless they left their village – or if Sonam was able to defy the odds and bring a school to them. But here in Nar it seemed as though there might be at least a sliver of hope for the children.

Taking the teacher up on his offer of a visit, Arek, Michael, Chantal and I made our way to the school the following morning. We found the tiny schoolhouse high up on the hillside, nestled near the outskirts of the village. I opened the rickety wooden gate, and together we entered the school courtyard, which overlooked the stark wall of Pisang Peak. Opposite to us, enclosing the courtyard, was a double L-shaped stone building with several classrooms. The rooms were dark, since the school had no electricity, and they were empty because the children were all outdoors, studying in the light and warmth of the sun. What must it be like in those rooms in the winter, I wondered.

In the centre of the square I counted 17 small children, ranging from 3 to 7 in age, sitting on wooden school benches they had dragged outside and placed in neat rows facing the "teacher": a little girl. Most of them were dressed in old raggedy clothes, but a handful wore school uniforms, dusty and frayed at the seams. The uniforms consisted of pants, most of which were so large they had to be hiked up around their tiny waists and held up by string, topped by navy blue sweaters worn over baby blue collared shirts. Black ties decorated with tiny white dots hung loosely around their necks. Some of the boys wore colourful wooly tuques with earflaps that draped over their shoulders. Others wore loosely fitting ball caps. Most of the girls had wrapped their heads in bright scarves of different colours. All the children had cheeks burnished a deep red by the sun, some of them so badly sunburned they had blisters on their faces. Many of them also seemed to be suffering from perpetual colds, with thick yellow snot dripping down their upper lips.

At the head of the courtyard, where we would have expected to see the schoolmaster Jason and Arek had met the previous day, was a child no taller than the chipped wood frame of the chalkboard behind her. It was she who was teaching the class. She was one of the children wearing a uniform, which, like the others, was frayed and worn. But it was obvious someone had put care into her appearance, for her clothes were clean, her baby blue collared shirt was tucked neatly into her oversized pants and her long dark hair was tightly braided and bound back with a bright orange head scarf. Small silver hooped earrings glittered beneath the scarf. Although she, too, had a forehead and cheeks scarred by sunburn, she was lit from within by a radiance that set her apart from her classmates. We had encountered hundreds of Himalayan children since we had set out several weeks ago, each adorable and engaging. Yet there was something different about this little girl. Somehow the mere sight of her pulled at my heart, and I felt a strange connection to her.

In her left hand, she was holding a white pencil and pointing it, one by one, to the numerals on the board. The numerals were written out in English script, which differs from the Nepali. She recited each number to the class with the poise and authority of someone teaching in a university auditorium, and the entire class followed her without missing a beat, repeating the numbers 1 through 70, in English, in unison. We watched as they went through their recitation, clearly articulating each of the numbers as seriously as if they were reading scripture, and then they started over.

In the rear of the courtyard I caught sight of a figure watching over the proceedings – the (real) schoolteacher. He looked out of place – not by way of his dress but because of his facial features. Unlike the Mongolian-looking faces around us, which are typical of the Bhotiya people of the northern reaches of the Himalaya, the schoolteacher's face was darker in skin tone, with rounder eyes and a broader nose. He came over to welcome us, smiling but with a kind of weariness that seemed to weigh him down. He did not look like a happy man. Arek and Jason had mentioned that he had told them he felt like he was in exile here in this remote part of the world. Since he was presumably from the educated class, and probably from one of the Hindu ethnic groups that are the majority in Nepal, it was likely he considered himself above the people he was living among. Nepal is very caste-conscious, and the Indigenous peoples of the north are considered inferior.

In halting English he explained that the lesson he was teaching today was focused on English, Nepali and mathematics – although from the looks of it, he wasn't teaching at all, having ceded his duties to the little girl at the chalkboard. He seemed indifferent to what was going on in his class, disengaged. Sonam had told us that postings in these remote villages were so undesirable that it was not uncommon for some of the teachers assigned to them to disappear altogether, while still collecting their salaries. The Nepali government had established the village schools, but they were simply too far away from the central authority to be monitored. As a result, the children lost their chance at an education, but no one seemed to care.

Soon the little girl had made it through all the English numbers for the second time, and it wasn't long before the children's attention turned to their visitors – in particular to the guitar slung over Michael's shoulder. They had likely never seen such an instrument, let alone heard the sounds from one. It piqued the teacher's interest as well, and he indicated by gesture that we were welcome to teach the kids a bit of music. Entertainer that he was, Michael didn't hesitate an instant to move to the front of the class. With a large grin on his face, he strummed a few opening chords. The children were captivated at once. All eyes were fixed on him as they eagerly awaited what would come next. Michael proceeded to teach the children the lyrics to "Twinkle, Twinkle, Little Star." But this was no ordinary version. It was a jazzed-up rendition – a fresh tempo with all sorts of unexpected melodic twists. Somehow the kids caught on, singing the lyrics back to the bard in perfect unison. And then Michael really put his guitar into action. Accompanied by the soft chorus of children's voices, he soon had the mountain classroom rocking to the rhythms of his songs.

The music even enlivened the schoolteacher, who brought out a traditional Nepali drum. He directed all the children except for one – the little girl who had been teaching the class – to organize themselves in a row. She apparently was expected to perform for us. After some brief commands in the Nepali language, he started to tap the edge of the drum with his hands, waiting for the child to demonstrate a traditional Nepali dance. But the little girl who had stood so proudly and confidently before her class seemed frozen. Now that she had been singled out from her peers and put in front of an audience of strangers she stood motionless, head bowed, hands clasped in front of her. When the teacher pulled her forward, she balked, looking like a petrified animal. But the teacher kept playing, while everyone else looked on, still waiting for her to dance. The longer this went on, the more distraught the little girl appeared.

Chantal couldn't take it any longer. Something stirred within her. Maybe it was the years of performance anxiety she herself had endured in her youth when she was training as a classical violinist. Maybe it was because she simply felt for the little girl, remembering a time when she, too, had been singled out against her wishes to perform in front of her classmates. Whatever the reason, Chantal suddenly marched forward and took her place in front of the child, focusing all of her attention on her. Slowly, she began to move her hips and wave her arms in the air. What ensued was a smorgasbord of dance moves. It was Chantal's best imitation of a traditional Nepali dance, and it would have to do.

The girl's eyes lit up in surprise as she watched Chantal. Her face relaxed into an expression of relief – she had been rescued. A smile came to her lips, revealing a missing baby tooth in the front and soft dimples in her cheeks. And then the girl followed Chantal's lead, watching her feet, her hips, her arms, as she meticulously attempted to imitate each one of Chantal's improvised moves. Chantal's eyes began to glow as their eyes locked into each other's. They danced side by side in their own world, like two spirits revelling in the joy of their movement and their connection to each other, before an audience of snow-clad Himalayan giants.

As the tapping from the teacher on his drum died down into silence, Chantal embraced the girl and, placing her hands under her arms, lifted her into the air in a gesture of triumph. In response, the girl held fast to Chantal's arms and her cautious smile erupted into a huge gap-toothed grin. From her face shone happiness so pure that it felt as though time itself had ceased to move.

FOURTEEN

Scarcely two hours after our return to the tea house, four small heads poked themselves around the corner of a stone wall in the courtyard, peering at us with curious eyes and erupting in fits of small giggles. Chantal and I motioned for the children to come over. Though they had shed their uniforms and were now dressed in worn, dirty hand-me-downs, ragged and faded, we recognized them as children from the school. It hadn't taken them long to find us.

Included in the group was the little girl whom Chantal had danced with. She still wore her bright orange head scarf but had replaced the top of her school uniform with a greenish beige sweater, unravelling at the ends of the sleeves. Around her wrist she wore a thin gold band and two single string bracelets. Two small beads of coral and a piece of turquoise dangled from her neck. Her beaming smile and bright brown eyes shone at us as she came running at a speed that would have left me winded at this elevation. She flung herself into Chantal's arms, and the two of them embraced as they had at her school. She then turned to me, and, tiny thing that she was, leapt with all her might into my arms, nearly knocking me over. It wasn't the force of her body that threw me, but rather the force of her love. In that fraction of a second, as her small hands grasped the back of my neck and I felt the beat of her heart against mine, the purpose of my journey became clear.

Suddenly, everything made sense. I understood why I wasn't meant to climb that mountain. Had I split off from the group and ended up reconnecting with them in Kathmandu, I wouldn't have come to Nar and would have missed meeting this child. The trust I had placed in the flow of events had led me to this moment, to a connection I had never felt before. It was so intense that I wondered if it was perhaps a connection from a previous life. I wasn't sure of my belief in that kind of thing, but since coming to Nepal, the universe seemed to be bombarding me with signs, one after another, of a karmic connection to this place and its people. Whatever the connection was, however far from my understanding, I believed in it. I looked to Chantal and knew at once that she shared the same feeling. There was a life force binding us to that child at the soul level.

The little girl's friends caught up to her and lay siege to us. They knew little English but knew enough to say, "Chocolate! Chocolate!" Once they realized we didn't have any chocolate, their excitement died down, and the little girl with the orange head scarf stepped forward once again.

"*Nam ke ho*?" Chantal asked the girl, inquiring her name in Nepali.

"Karma."

My eyes met Chantal's. It nearly floored us. Of course, her name was Karma.

I asked Karma how old she was. She held up seven fingers.

She then proceeded to pull a small thin object from the breast pocket of the blouse beneath her sweater. It was a tattered laminated card bearing English words, with the picture of an object to illustrate the meaning of each word. She pointed to the first picture and then put her fingers to her mouth to indicate she wanted Chantal to teach her how to say the English words. Karma didn't want chocolate. She didn't need chocolate. All she wanted was to learn.

After Karma and her friends left us that day, Chantal and I sprung into motion. Accompanied by Devi, who would act as our translator, we asked as many Nepalis as we could their views on education, and whether they thought it was important for children in remote mountain villages like this one. We asked some of the members of our team, including, of course, Devi, as well as Dawa and IC, who had children of his own. We also spoke to the owner of the local tea house where we stayed, who also had kids, and several of the other villagers as well. We learned many things that day.

We learned that children from Nar could only get a full Nepali government education if they left the village. Some whose parents were fortunate enough to have the resources (such as the owner of the tea house where we were staying) would send their kids to school in one of the larger villages along the Annapurna Circuit, or to a Tibetan boarding school in Kathmandu. Parents who didn't have the money but did want their children to be educated would send them off to a monastery before they reached the age of 10. There they would study to become nuns or monks. While this would mean devoting themselves to a life of service to the monastery, at least they would get a full education and three meals a day. Children who did not leave the village would inevitably become farmers, the girls marrying as young as 14 or 15 and having children of their own soon thereafter.

Chantal and I wanted to meet Karma's family. We had to sit down with them and understand their plans for the future of this bright young girl who had such passion and thirst to learn. It was clear to us now that, if Karma stayed in Nar, her prospects for education would be next to nil. The village school scratched the surface of Grade 1, and, bright, eager student that she was, she had probably already mastered all it had to offer. I asked Dawa to find out where she lived, and he disappeared into the village. After Dawa left, Chantal and I found Karma and her friends and spent the rest of the afternoon playing with them. A couple rounds of tag left the two of us panting for air, as Karma and her friends ran circles around us, giggling their heads off. Remembering a game I had played with my 5-year-old niece back home in Canada, one she'd aptly named "rocket ship," I caught up with Karma, and, lifting her in my arms, I held on tightly and ran with her around the field. She soared through the air, light as a feather. Racing around while carrying her left me gasping, but Karma's delight was worth it. I noticed that around other men Karma was wary and kept her distance. However, with me she was completely comfortable – as though there was a familial bond between us.

Taking a break to catch my breath, I sat next to Chantal on a stone partition and we watched Karma play with her friends. Chantal had a look of sheer joy in her eyes.

"Mike, I think I've known this for a while. I need to find a way to spend less time in front of the computer. Less time at the rat race and have more one-on-one human connection. More time with our families. And I really think we need to move out of the city and be closer to nature."

I nodded in agreement. I didn't need any convincing. Shortly after we'd finished our undergraduate degrees, Chantal and I had moved to the city of Vancouver and into a downtown condo. For nine years we had lived the city life, one we had fully embraced throughout our 20s. However, being out here, disconnected from all the noise and rush and ambition of the city, gave us the chance to find a new rhythm, a new way of being. It reminded us of what was important.

"Mike, that hug Karma gave me when she found us this afternoon – that was the biggest, deepest hug I've ever gotten from a child."

"Me too. There's something about her. Somehow I feel a love for her. It's the same love I imagine I would feel for my own daughter."

"Mike, are we crazy – what we're doing here?"

"Yes. I don't know where it's all going. But something just *feels* right about it."

Without ever having put it into words, Chantal and I seemed to have decided we wanted to try to help Karma get an education.

Karma and her friends had defaulted to a different game – one that involved each of them putting a rock in one shoe and chasing each other around. It wasn't clear how the game worked, but it certainly looked like they were having fun. Observing the village children, we found it remarkable how good they were at entertaining themselves, creating their own games from nothing but sticks and stones. Yet they never forgot their responsibilities. Wherever they went, they always seemed to bring a toddler or two with them, and they'd take turns watching the little ones, while their parents worked long hours herding their yaks in the mountains and cultivating the fields.

It was getting close to 6:00 p.m., and Karma and her friends disappeared from our view just as Dawa returned with the good news. Dawa had found her home and arranged for us to visit Karma's mother there in another hour or so, after she'd returned from working in the fields.

In the meantime, Devi and Dawa brought Chantal and me to the locals' tea house where we could wait. It was a small dark room, smelling of soot and earth, and consisted of nothing more than a bar, a miniature, wood-burning stove and a few short-legged stools, with scarcely enough space for the four of us to sit. We saw our young Sherpa Umang loitering in a corner. He broke out in a large, almost sheepish grin as we entered – and as soon as I saw the young girl behind the bar I understood why. I gave him a knowing, conspiratorial smile, but he wouldn't meet my eyes. His gaze shifted to the floor, and his face flushed a deep red. Dawa later told me that Umang had met the young girl on a previous expedition to Nar several months ago and the two seemed to like each other – though so far, Dawa said, shaking his head in amusement and chuckling, their relationship consisted of nothing more than a few words and fleeting moments of eye contact over the space of nearly half a year's time.

The young girl served us hot butter tea as we waited. Absorbed by the flickering amber glow of the fireplace, I sipped the hot liquid slowly and listened with half an ear to Devi, Dawa and Umang bantering in Nepali. They clearly enjoyed themselves much more here than in Phu. Chantal in the meantime had gulped down her butter tea. It was her first cup, and I had forgotten to warn her about the instant refill problem. The young girl came by to replenish Chantal's cup to the brim, and when I saw the strange look on Chantal's face as she tried to suppress her dismay and force an expression of thanks to her lips, I realized why Jason had nearly burst out laughing at my reaction in the longhouse in Koto.

Before long, 7:00 rolled around and it was time for us to go. Chantal and I were nervous about meeting Karma's family, unsure what we would say to them. As we exited the tea house, we encountered none other than Karma herself, still beaming that bright smile of hers. She took Chantal by the hand, and with Devi, Dawa and I trailing behind, Karma led us down the narrow village pathways. We wound this way and that, until I had lost track of where we were amid the labyrinth of stone houses. Upon passing a large stone chorten and the village mani wall, a much less imposing one than the mani wall at the entrance to the village, we arrived at the entrance of Karma's home, which was framed by a small wooden gate. Ducking under a low beam and stepping over the lip of the threshold, I was immediately hit with the strong, familiar smell of earth and soot. As my eyes adjusted, I saw that the house was similar to Sonam's in Phu. It was a single room with four walls of earth and rock, dimly lit by the light from a single opening in the wall that served as a window. In the middle of the room was a dung-fuelled stove. Against one wall were shelves with all their belongings, mainly dishes and cooking pots. Dried strips of yak meat hung from the centre of the room, and on a side table there was a single basket with a few hand-me-down stuffed teddy bears that had seen better days.

Karma welcomed us in. Her mother was still working in the field. It was now well past 7:00, and she had likely left for the fields at dawn that day. Karma pulled out some mats and wool rugs for us to sit on. She then placed a water kettle on the stove and began to prepare the fire. She did all this while looking after her 3-year-old sister, a beautiful little girl named Pemba, who was running around the room in excitement over their visitors. I recognized the little one from the school. During our time there she had scarcely left Karma's side. Once Karma was satisfied that she had made us at home, she dashed off to fetch her mother, leaving us behind with her little sister, who seemed to take a great interest in chatting with Devi.

Devi was much charmed by Pemba. "This little one," he said with a grin and a chuckle, "very, very clever!"

Before long, Karma returned, together with her mother and another woman, Lhakpa, who was introduced as one of Karma's sisters. Karma's mother, Pema, was a graceful, beautiful woman with deep eyes and high cheekbones, but her bronze face, leathered and worn from many years of exposure to the sun, made her look ten years older than she was. She wore a traditional thick chuba dress and a necklace of two chunks of coral around a piece of turquoise. A dusty beige scarf held her dark hair behind her, revealing her large brass hooped earrings. She welcomed us as warmly as Karma had and, without knowing anything about her new guests, immediately proceeded to prepare butter tea for us, which she mixed in a large wooden cylinder. As Pema pushed the wooden mixer into the cylinder, assessing Chantal and me with her gentle yet watchful eyes, Devi explained who we were, and that we were interested to learn about Karma and what the family had planned for her education. After the butter tea concoction was ready, Pema poured each of her guests a cup and then one for herself. This time Chantal nursed her cup as carefully as I did, to forestall the customary top-up.

With Devi acting as our translator, we learned Pema and her husband had six daughters, the oldest of whom was Lhakpa, now 24, and that Karma and little Pemba were the youngest. Pema laughed when she told us she had given birth to Pemba at the age of 44, as though she could still hardly believe it herself. Lhakpa had stayed in the village and married, but did not have any kids. She had the voice of a child and looked as strong as an ox. Though she had the same attractive features as Karma and Pemba, the hard life of the mountains had begun to take its toll. She looked more like a woman in her mid-30s than mid-20s. The next two daughters, Nyima and Wangyal, ages 18 and 16, had been sent off to an abbey near Kathmandu to become nuns. The fourth oldest, Palma, who was 9, was studying in a remote school outside of Pokhara. There were no plans for Karma and Pemba.

Pema told us that her husband, Sonam, was far away, higher in the mountains, tending to their herd of yaks, and would not be back for at least a couple of days. As Chantal and I had declared our interest to Devi earlier in the day about sponsoring Karma's education, he did not waste time in raising the question to Pema about the future of Karma's education. We then learned the thing we most wanted to know: that for Pema and Sonam, the education of their children was the greatest blessing they could hope for, and they were prepared to send their daughters as far away as need be to get it.

"Devi," I asked, "please ask Karma if she would like to pursue her education."

Devi translated my words, to which Karma's eyes immediately lit up, and with a hopeful smile, she spoke a few words affirming her desire to study.

"Then please tell them that, for as long as Karma would like to study, we will provide for her education."

As Devi translated my words, I looked to Karma's mother, trying to gauge her reaction. Pema looked to me and then Chantal and nodded slowly. She was clearly moved by our offer and grateful for it, and at the same time seemed to be weighing everything that had just occurred in her mind.

As it was getting late, we told them we were to leave Nar tomorrow morning, but that if it was all right with them, we would return in the morning for one more visit before our departure. Pema agreed to see us again the next day, her kind eyes ever resting on Chantal and me.

Back at the tea house where we were staying, we rendezvoused with Michael and Arek, who were curious about where we had disappeared to. Following our visit to the school, all of us had gone our separate ways, so they had no idea of what had transpired with Karma. Words began to pour nonstop from us. Chantal and I were so overwhelmed that we had hardly spoken about it even to each other, and now Arek and Michael were the first to receive the full download. We told them about Karma and her friends finding us after school, and about how we'd seen Karma's yearning to learn. We told them how blown away we'd been when we'd found out that her name was *Karma*, and about the deep, karmic connection the three of us felt for each other. We rattled off all the information we'd gathered from the locals – about their remote village life, and how they viewed education, and the great lengths they would have to go to send their children to school. We shared everything we had learned about Karma's family, her sisters and her mother and father. And I reflected on my own realization that, by losing my chance at the pyramid mountain, I had gained something much more valuable, which brought new meaning to the decision I'd made. Now I saw that it had all been for a purpose. Michael and Arek listened to this outpouring with utter bewilderment and fascination.

While we were still in the midst of our story, in strolled Jason, the cowboy, sunburnt and red-cheeked, who was returning from his own day's adventure. While the rest of us had visited the school, he'd gone off that morning in search of the Himalayan griffons, which he wanted to sketch. All conversation stopped dead for a moment when we saw him, and Jason, puzzled by the sudden silence, looked at us as if he thought we might be planning a bank heist.

"What? What did I miss?"

The following morning we awoke to the sun. It shone warmly, perhaps the warmest it had since our journey began. Chantal and I had hardly slept that night – running over and over again what had happened and trying to make sense of it all. After packing faster than we'd ever packed before, because we didn't want to lose any time with Karma and her family, we headed back to their home, accompanied again by Devi, who could translate for us. Following the same winding pathways, we kept an eye out for the village mani wall, so we'd be able to recognize Karma's house. Just as we approached the wooden gate, Karma, who'd clearly been watching for us, burst through it and launched herself into my arms once again. I held her tiny frame tightly before letting her go. Karma turned and ran back into the house, followed by Chantal, Devi and me.

Pema and Lhakpa were waiting for us. They had prepared hot butter tea, along with deep-fried crackers called *chhurpi*, made from the milk of female yaks. Both mother and daughter seemed pleased and happy to see us. It appeared as though Karma's family had come to some sort of a consensus during the night, and that they were fully ready to trust Chantal and me with Karma's future. As we had no idea when we would see each other again, Chantal reached into her wallet and pulled out the only photo of ourselves we had with us – a small photo from our wedding day. She handed Karma the picture, but before she could even get a look at it, little Pemba ran by like a rocket and snatched the photo from Karma's hands, studying it intensely. Devi couldn't help laughing. "That little one. So clever!"

After we'd exchanged mailing addresses, Pema took out two beige silk *khatas*, traditional Tibetan scarves, and placed one on my shoulders, the other on Chantal's. She then unwrapped a third, a white one, and carefully tied it around Karma's neck and shoulders. Although we could not speak each other's languages, I understood this gesture had some kind of significance, and learned later that such scarves are given as gifts on ceremonial occasions. If given to say farewell, they symbolize the wish for a safe journey. As I gazed into the depths of Pema's eyes, I felt a swell of emotions. I was in awe of the generosity and hospitality that had been offered to us, and deeply moved by the trust Karma's mother had bestowed upon two people who only a day before were complete strangers to her. Some part of me didn't want to leave. I wanted to stay there in their home and get to know them. Our visit had been far too short. There was so much more to learn about this family and their ways.

And then, without knowing how we would fulfill the promise we had made to the family for Karma's education, and unsure if or when we would ever see each other again, we bid each other farewell.

After rendezvousing with our group back at the tea house, we set forth on our journey back to Kathmandu, and home. We passed through the Nar gate, walking alongside the grand mani wall that had taken our breath away when we had first entered the village. Yet, as momentous as that entrance had been, it could not possibly have prepared me for the life-changing events Nar had in store for me. Nor could I possibly have anticipated how painful it would be to say goodbye to Nar.

Leaving the mountain behind had been difficult. Leaving Karma was something else altogether. Each step we took was a step further away from her, and a step into increasing uncertainty. Chantal and I had no idea what we would be able to do for Karma. Would we be able to find her a suitable school in Nepal, and if so how far would she have to travel, and would she be able to adapt to life outside her village and away from her family? Would we have to search beyond Nepal? Would it be possible for her to come to Canada to study? And even if it was, and we could get the right permits and papers, would this be the best thing for Karma? What would it mean for Karma to leave her country?

I seemed to be lost in a sea of confusion, with no idea of where the path would lead. But if there was one thing I had learned in these last few weeks, it was to trust in the flow of events unfolding around me. For it was only in trusting and opening myself up to whatever was to come that I'd received the gift of meeting Karma.

The glittering peaks of Nar towered over me as all this ran through my head. I tilted the brim of my cap upwards to take one last look at them, and, with a new-found joy in my heart, I bid them farewell.

FIFTEEN

We had nearly given up hope. Weeks of searching went by, and Chantal and I could not find a suitable school for Karma. We had searched during our remaining days in Kathmandu, and we continued searching long after returning to Canada. Days turned into weeks, and weeks soon became a month. The problem wasn't finding a school in Nepal; it was finding the right school in Nepal. It was imperative to find a school that would honour Karma's Tibetan Buddhist roots and her ethnic and cultural heritage, which were vastly different from the predominantly Hindu culture of Nepal.

We also sought a school that would help her transition from remote village life into the bigger world around her. She had scarcely been outside a five-kilometre radius from her village, which had a population of around 700 people. She hadn't even seen a bicycle before, let alone experienced a big chaotic city like Kathmandu, with its cars and motorbikes and a population of some 1.5 million people. And, on top of this, the school would have to provide a safe environment for boarding students. Many of the schools we encountered were either large government schools with large class sizes and a mostly Hindu cultural orientation, or private schools that were likely to be filled with students from high-ranking Hindu castes and the children of expats. We knew enough to understand that most of Nepal still operated on the caste system, and that the mountain people, who were from the Buddhist minority and could be easily identified as such by name and appearance, would be looked down on and discriminated against if not in the right environment.

And then, during one of Chantal's late-night searches, Google finally came to the rescue. "Mike, you have to check this out!" Chantal's eyes were fixed on her computer screen. Up popped the website for the Shree Mangal Dvip Boarding School. The school was located in the Kathmandu valley and situated near the great Boudhanath Stupa, a major Buddhist pilgrimage site that was the largest and easily the most glorious chorten in the world.

At the top of the page was a picture of Tibetan-looking children, snotty-nosed and sunburnt, clad in tattered clothes – looking just like the children we'd seen in the remote villages of Nar and Phu. "Education for the forgotten children of the high Himalaya of Nepal," read the photo caption. The school was founded in 1987 by the Venerable Khenchen Thrangu Rinpoche, the ninth incarnation of the great Thrangu tulku. (We had no idea what this meant at the time, but it sounded impressive.) Thrangu Rinpoche is a high-ranking lama born in Tibet in 1933, who fled to India in 1959. He had since built monasteries all over the world and founded the Shree Mangal Dvip Boarding School – SMD – specifically for the children in the upper Nepal Himalayan belt. These were the children from some of the most inaccessible, impoverished parts of Nepal, the ones who fell through the cracks. They came from isolated places with no roads, electricity, running water, sanitation, telecommunication, health care or schools. Places like where Karma was from.

SMD's kids were Tibetan in culture and Buddhist in thinking, and Thrangu Rinpoche's mission was to enrich secular education with that of the Tibetan and Himalayan culture. The secular curriculum was based on that of the Nepali government, but in addition to that the school aimed to teach the tenets of Tibetan Buddhism, including prayer and meditation, in order to keep the Buddhist way of life of the Himalayas alive. Once the children graduate, at the tenth grade level, they are encouraged to continue their education in the fields of health and education so they can return to their villages and communities and help them. Thrangu Rinpoche wanted both to preserve the Buddhist way of life in the high Himalaya and improve village life so their people would be better equipped to sustain themselves. It sounded as though he was trying to address all the issues Sonam Dorje was so concerned about in Phu. SMD sounded perfect for Karma.

We wrote the school at once, describing our experience in Nar, and the little girl we had met there, whose passion to learn and study had so impressed us. We poured our hearts out in our email, going into great detail about our encounter, even down to a description of Chantal and Karma dancing together, and our discovery of a deep karmic connection with each other.

A week went by, during which we waited on tenterhooks, before we received a reply from the school's director, Shirley Blair. Her email was kind, sympathetic and heartfelt. She acknowledged the profound experience we'd had with Karma and the remarkable qualities we had observed in her character. She then proceeded to tell us about the school – that it was bursting at the seams. That it had over 500 students and another 400 on the waitlist. That even one of the local lama's nephews couldn't get a placement. That it had children being dropped off on its doorstep only to turn them away. It was heart-wrenching to read. Finally, Shirley wrote, on top of all this, there is only one person who admits new children to the school. And this was none other than the founder himself, the Venerable Thrangu Rinpoche.

Reading through Shirley's response felt like being dropped down a black hole, just as we thought we were close to finding the solution. It was as though every possible barrier was stacked against this one little girl, someone who so richly deserved a fighting chance at an education. I began to feel dejected by the whole situation. That is, until we read the last line of Shirley's email, which I will never forget: "P.S. I see that you live in Vancouver. You may be interested to know that Venerable Thrangu Rinpoche happens to be at his monastery in Richmond, BC, right now, recovering from an illness." Chantal and I looked at each other in disbelief. That was a 30-minute drive from our home.

SIXTEEN

Strings of colourful prayer flags, just like the ones we had seen in Nepal, streamed forth from the centre crown of the monastery. The tall brick building was adorned with finely crafted, intricately detailed woodcarvings and topped with a pagoda-style golden roof that shone brilliantly beneath the sun.

We approached the stairs that led to the monastery's front entrance. Tashi led the way. Tashi was a young woman whom Shirley at the Shree Mangal Dvip Boarding School had introduced us to via email. A young woman from a remote mountain village in the Gorkha district of northern Nepal, a place very similar to where Karma lived, Tashi had been admitted to the SMD school at a young age, along with her sister Nangsal. The two of them had subsequently been able to come to Canada on scholarship to finish their high school and university degrees. Being with Tashi brought us right back to Nar. She had the same deep brown cat-like eyes, bronze-coloured skin and dark flowing hair that the people of Nar did. Petite in stature yet imposing in bearing, she reminded us of so many of the mountain dwellers we had met in the Himalaya.

When we first met Tashi, and shared our story of Karma with her, tears welled in her eyes, and she insisted she would bring us to Thrangu Rinpoche's monastery. She was sure we would be able to get in.

Entering together, we were greeted by a monk who was the chief administrator at the monastery. He inquired about the purpose of our visit, and I told him we were there to see Thrangu Rinpoche. Caught off guard by such an audacious request, he answered sharply, saying Thrangu

Rinpoche was ill and not seeing anyone. He then asked why we wanted to see Thrangu Rinpoche. I couldn't help myself, so I regaled the young monk with our story of Karma. His eyes softened and I could see something shifting inside. He looked at Tashi. "Why don't you take them for a tour of the monastery, and then come back."

Entering the main shrine hall of the monastery was like being transported back to Nepal. The smell of incense, the vibrant colours, the monks, the calm energy of the place – it was as if they had beamed an entire building and all its properties and monks out of Nepal straight into Canada. It felt good to be back in this culture. There was a strange sense of homecoming about it.

When we returned to the front desk, the young monk approached us. "I have telephoned upstairs. Thrangu Rinpoche will see you now. You'll have five minutes with him."

It all happened so fast. I don't think I quite grasped the magnitude of what was occurring. Tashi began shaking like a leaf. Thrangu Rinpoche was her guru. He was the one who had made her education possible, who had given her a future. But this would be the first time she had ever had a private audience with him. Chantal also began to tremble. "Mike, you're doing the talking," she whispered.

Thrangu Rinpoche was one of the most prominent figures among the leaders of Tibetan Buddhism. In his 900-year-old lineage, the Karma Kagyu, he was second only to the Seventeenth Karmapa, who many believe will assume the leadership of the Tibetan Buddhist people upon the passing of the current Dalai Lama. The Seventeenth Karmapa was much younger than Thrangu Rinpoche, so His Holiness the Dalai Lama had asked Thrangu Rinpoche to serve as the teacher and mentor to the young Karmapa.

We climbed the stairs while the young monk explained to us how to greet the Venerable Thrangu Rinpoche, what to do when we entered the room and how to behave. He gave each of us a khata, a silk scarf like the one Karma's mother had given us, which we were to present to Thrangu Rinpoche. And then we were standing before the man we had come to see, scarcely able to believe this was happening.

I had heard there are people who can see the auras of others, but I myself had never seen anyone glow – until that moment. It was as though there was a soft white force field around Thrangu Rinpoche, a lightness that radiated from everything he touched. His dark eyes were profound in their depth, as if his pupils were bottomless. His smile was warm, his demeanour gentle. In addition to all of this was the feeling he inspired – as if being in his presence exposed the light of my soul. The old lama, wrapped in his burgundy robe, lay in a modest bed, propped up by a few pillows.

"*Tashi delek.*" Each of us greeted him with this blessing as one by one we presented him with the khatas, which he in turn placed over our heads, along with a single string of beads that he put around each of our wrists. We then sat on mats arranged in a crescent around his bed. To my left was Chantal, to my right Tashi. The young monk, who would act as our translator, knelt on the floor beside Thrangu Rinpoche.

When he asked what had brought us to him, I didn't think of what to say. Words just started flowing from my mouth, and I began telling him everything – about my dream to climb the pyramidal mountain in the Himalaya and how events had worked against me and instead brought us to Nar, which led us to the little school, which led us to meeting Karma. After every few sentences, I would pause and wait for the young monk to translate. Thrangu Rinpoche did not speak during this outpouring. His eyes remained on me as he listened. I explained in great detail our experience at the school. How Karma had taught her class the English numbers, how Chantal had rescued Karma from the dance – this elicited a chuckle from Thrangu Rinpoche – and how Karma had found us after school. I went on about how she didn't ask for chocolate like all her friends but simply wanted us to teach her English words. I described Karma's home and her mother, explaining there were six sisters in their family, two of whom were nuns, and said how much her family valued education. I recounted it so vividly it was as though it had happened the day before, and spoke with so much feeling it was as though I was pleading a case for a little girl's life – which was how it felt to me. It took about 15 minutes for me to tell the story in its entirety, and I should have wondered if I was going on for too long, but I was in such a frenzy of emotion that I didn't. And Thrangu Rinpoche's attention never wavered.

When I finished the story, and the young monk had finished translating the last sentence, Thrangu Rinpoche sat there looking at me, and I at him, his eyes like a dark universe into which my own gaze flowed. After what seemed like minutes, but was probably only seconds, he spoke just a few words in Tibetan. I could feel my heartbeat accelerate, as I waited to find out what he had said. The young monk looked at me, then at Chantal and then back at me. "Thrangu Rinpoche says this year school is full. But that next year, beginning in April, Karma will be admitted into SMD."

Something within me moved – turned somersaults, really. It hadn't sunk in yet, but I knew we had done it. And then Thrangu Rinpoche propped himself up a little higher, and, staring into my eyes, asked one question – in English: "What do you do?"

I inadvertently let out a somewhat strangled laugh. In that moment the world I lived and worked in – the world of finance and investments – made no sense. Here was a man who had dedicated his life (and eight lifetimes before it) to the exploration and understanding of the inner world of spiritual consciousness, and to serving the world through love and compassion. What could the world of capitalism, of money, wealth and consumerism, possibly mean to him? While Western society has devoted itself to the accumulation of material goods, the Tibetan Buddhists have devoted themselves for thousands of years to achieving inner peace and harmony. The contrast blindsided me. Yet I answered him, and he nodded with a smile, as though he understood what I was thinking.

Then we stood, and, still facing the old lama, we backed away slowly with our hands at our chest in prayer position and exited the room. The glow of his aura left my sight, yet inside myself I felt something new stirring deep within my heart.

SEVENTEEN

I never had any intention of majoring in business in university. In fact, my goal was to major in creative writing. Throughout high school, English and math had been my best subjects, but it was writing I really loved. It ignited a flame within me like no other subject. As soon as the English teacher gave us our essay and short story assignments, I would race home, rush up into my room and begin to write feverishly, often for hours at a time. These early efforts were much praised, and the teacher would often read my work to the class.

And then I entered university. I'll never forget my first assignment: write a one-page essay describing a place in the outdoors that has deeply affected you. With my love for mountains and hiking, this was the assignment of my dreams, and I knew just the spot I would write about – a forested hill overlooking the entire peninsula where I'd grown up, and a place where my father and I would hike together. Upon completing the essay, I looked it over, and looked it over again. It was the best piece of work I had ever written. I was sure of it.

Two weeks later, we got our graded assignments back. I couldn't wait to see what the professor had written. But when I looked, my mind couldn't quite register what it was seeing – a letter that was so unfamiliar to me I was sure I wasn't reading it correctly. But I was. It was the letter *F*. I had failed. And that was more or less the end of my interest in taking creative writing classes at university.

Fortunately, the end of that passion coincided with the beginning of something else. My self-started business was suddenly picking up momentum. A few years earlier, upon graduating from Grade 10, I had travelled to Europe to visit my father's hometown of Solingen, Germany. As a 15-year-old kid, I was in love with medieval swords. Solingen was famous for steel craftsmanship. Give a resident of Solingen a hunk of steel, and he would create an artistic masterpiece from it. My cousin, who lived in Solingen, and I toured the city. We were on a quest to find an authentic blacksmith who still forged swords, which turned out not to be so easy.

As the internet was just in its infancy, we couldn't just perform a Google search, and had to investigate on foot. After several days, we finally found a smithy in a nondescript warehouse, down a flight of concrete stairs, in a space where the smell of fire, brimstone and cold steel immediately singed my lungs. The clash of hammers on metal rang throughout the warehouse. There was fire. There was iron. There were massive blocks of steel dropping into flames. I stood there dumbfounded. A large man, presumably the owner, left his desk and approached us. He towered over me. His forearms were as wide as my thighs. His thick handlebar moustache draped down his chin, and his blue apron was stained with soot and grease. His steel-toed boots looked as though each weighed five kilograms. He couldn't speak much English, so my cousin tried as best she could to explain why a scrawny kid from Canada looking for a sword had interrupted his work. And then something totally unexpected happened. The German giant reached behind his desk and, as though picking up a feather-light stick, retrieved a one-metre-long masterpiece of a blade. He handled it as though it was a rapier. But the blade was thick. The steel was etched with eye-squintingly intricate detail. The hilt was bound with dried fish skin and wrapped with braided steel thread. The cross guard was a tangled, hollowed half-moon of finely carved vines. It was by far the most striking sword I had seen. And then the man, apparently touched by the presence of a kid who had travelled halfway around the world to find him, handed me the sword. "A gift," he said.

I was unable to speak. I couldn't believe he had just given me that sword. In his broken English, he then asked me a question that would change my life course. "Do you think others in Canada, like my swords?"

My eyes met his, and with no hesitation I answered, "Hell, yes."

I had a plan. For the remainder of my trip I could scarcely contain myself. As soon as I returned to Canada, I would start a business and begin to import his swords. There was nowhere you could find such artistic works of steel in Canada. It was brilliant. As soon as I got off the plane, I explained my plan to my parents, and as they had so often done before, they wholeheartedly supported my wild idea.

My mom drove me around for the next couple days since I was too young to drive. We went to the tariff office to learn about duties on swords. We went to the business registrar to get my Goods and Services Tax number, register my business name and get a business number. She drove me to the local stationery store so I could get business cards made up and printed. And then, with my sword in hand, a handful of business cards, and wearing one of my dad's old ties, I began going around to stores I thought might be interested in buying Solingen-made steel blades.

"I'll see you in an hour," my dad would say as he dropped me off. And although the business owners were kind and I learned a lot about how to do business from them, I never sold a single sword. But somehow back in Solingen word was getting around about a Canadian import operation, and manufacturers from that small industrial city began contacting me. Most of them didn't know I lived in a sleepy island suburb of Victoria, let alone that I was just a kid, nor did they seem to know the difference between Canada and the United States. To them, it was all the New World of North America, and they thought I might be their big break into the US. Armed with the dozens of catalogues and samples they began sending me in the mail – everything from hair salon scissors and sewing scissors to kitchen and hunting knives and manicure sets – I started making sales calls again. And this time, unlike my failed attempt at selling swords, I found buyers who actually liked my high-quality steel products. I was soon selling to stores throughout my home province of British Columbia.

One day I received a big box of stainless steel designer kitchenware. I peeled through the box of stainless steel sieves, basting brushes, tongs, graters and an assortment of other articles. It all seemed kind of boring. After all, at my age anything to do with the kitchen was totally uninteresting to me. "Why don't you just take them to a few kitchen stores and see what they think?" my dad suggested. Heck, what did I have to lose?

Unbeknownst to me, this was a time – the mid-1990s – when kitchens had become no longer just a place to cook. The kitchen was now the social hub for the household. People were renovating their homes by knocking down walls and putting as much effort and money into the appearance of their kitchens as they would their living rooms or dining rooms. After remodelling their kitchen, they would look for new utensils that were as elegant in design as they were functional. This was before stainless steel became widely available, with most kitchenware still being made out of plastic, so my wares were much in demand. My business was about to go through the roof.

Over the next few years, my business went national, and I began distributing designer stainless steel kitchenware across the country. We converted my parents' garage into a warehouse. My dad came out of retirement to manage the office and shipments, and I even hired a sales rep.

Meanwhile, back at university I was struggling to get anything better than a B+ on my English assignments. Often, I had to skip class or leave early to deal with inventory management, currency trades or new customer inquiries. I was excited about expanding my business, and totally frustrated by my university experience, which seemed to be all about trying to shove me into a box.

And then I learned about the business school, where the faculty seemed much more open-minded, less academic. They weren't interested in boxes but in the opposite – in being receptive to possibility, innovation, creative thinking and change. Since I was already running a fairly successful business, and felt it was something I was good at, I switched majors and launched myself full-time into studying the world of commerce, while also working in it.

I didn't make a fortune off my first business, but it was enough to pay for my education and a down payment on my first home. More importantly for my future, through the business school curriculum I learned about investing, and on my own I began studying companies with an analytic eye. What made them great? Why were a handful of them widely successful, while most were mediocre at best? How was the success of a business reflected in its share prices? I wanted to put what I was learning into practice, so when I was only about 19 I opened a discount broker-age account and began trading my first positions. It was challenging. But it was also rewarding and exhilarating. I never looked back, nor did I ever question why I was doing it – that is, until I came face to face with the Venerable Thrangu Rinpoche.

EIGHTEEN

The tiny buildings, a mash-up of thousands of colourful, tightly packed structures, each no more than a few stories high and angled every which way, sprawled out to the horizon like a collage that gradually disappeared into the hazy green hills beyond. Peering out the airplane window as we descended, I found it hard to believe that Chantal and I were returning to Kathmandu only one year since making our first trip there. When we arrived that first time, almost exactly a year earlier, we had no idea we would be coming back again so soon. And yet here we were, having made the trip to be with Karma for her first days at the Shree Mangal Dvip Boarding School.

The year that had passed since we said goodbye to Karma and her family had seemed both much shorter and much longer than it actually was – shorter because there was so much to be done, longer because we missed Karma so much. During our time back in Vancouver, we had succeeded at the hardest challenge, which was to find an appropriate school and get Karma admitted, but in those 12 months there had been many other things we needed to accomplish as well. First came the task of communicating with Karma's family that we had found a school for her. It was essential that her parents give their consent to this, since Karma would be boarding in Kathmandu, a six-day journey from their village, most of it on foot. As there was no reliable postal service in Nepal, nor any means of telephoning Karma's family, we contacted our trusted Sherpa, Dawa, who agreed to deliver the message for us and act as our liaison. Dawa travelled a full day by bus and hiked for five days to relay our message. Then, of course, he had to repeat the journey on the way back. The answer he received from Karma's family, as well as from Karma herself, was an enthusiastic yes.

Months later, in the middle of a cold February night, I received a call over Facebook from a gentleman, Dawa Tashi, whom I'd never heard of. He explained that he was a monk at the monastery in Nar Phedi, and Karma's older cousin. Because his English was poor, and our signal was spotty, it was hard to understand him, but eventually I was able to make out that he and Karma had just made the six-day journey down to Kathmandu in the hope that she could start school early. But the school had turned them away since Karma wasn't due to arrive until two months later, and they didn't have a bed for her.

Chantal and I immediately went into a panic, picturing this little 8-year-old girl stranded in the chaos of Kathmandu. She would never have seen anything like the city, and for all we knew she and Dawa Tashi had nowhere to stay. We reached out to all the contacts we had, but in the end the only option was for Karma and her cousin to make the long trek back up to her village and return again in April.

Once again, we were seeing the Nepali way in action. Plans were never seamless; nothing could be forced. One simply had to adapt and flow with the ever-evolving course of events. But now it was April, and Dawa Tashi had brought Karma down to the school again. We had arrived in time to see her on her first day there.

Being in Kathmandu this time somehow didn't seem as much of a shock. The mayhem in the streets, the incessant blowing of car and bike horns, the millions of people heading this way and that, the smells of burning garbage and rotting sewage, the narrow dusty streets and the vibrantly alive markets – it all seemed both strange yet comfortingly familiar. However, we were eager to see Karma and wasted no time heading to her school, which is located in Boudha, once a quiet suburb of Kathmandu.

Though it has now been enveloped in the ever-expanding hustle and bustle of the capital, Boudha still maintains some of its former peacefulness. Cobblestone streets wind their way around in a labyrinth that is centred on the great Boudha Stupa, an immense, historic structure – variously believed to have been built as early as the 5th century and as late as the 14th – which is at the very heart of the community. Cement and brick buildings line the streets, each building tightly packed against the next. Home to a large population of Tibetans who fled their country after the Chinese insurgence in 1959, Boudha feels almost like an outpost of Tibet. Monks and nuns in burgundy robes swarm the streets, there are prayer wheels and prayer flags everywhere you look, Buddhist monasteries and stupas are scattered throughout and the many shops sell all manner of traditional Tibetan crafts, clothes and ceremonial items. Seeing it made me feel very good about the choice we had made for Karma, because it seemed like a place that would welcome her and be culturally compatible with her background.

Finding Karma's school took some time, as the streets all seemed to run into each other and building numbers were nonexistent. After asking several locals, many of whom simply looked at us in puzzlement, either because they didn't understand our pronunciation of the school's name or because they didn't know where it was, we eventually came to a tall green metal gate, topped with iron spires. I knocked on it and before long a small window in the gate opened. We explained we were there to see Shirley Blair, the school's director. The window closed, and a moment later we heard the sound of a metal wheel turning and, with a squeak and a clunk, the gate opened, revealing another world inside.

Removed from the incessant frenzy of Kathmandu, from its sewage- and garbage-infested streets and its sickly beggars, was a courtyard filled with beautiful children. Chantal and I stood there taking it all in. The jubilant sound of 500 children, brought together in this place from villages like Karma's in the high Himalaya, echoed throughout the schoolyard. No longer burdened by the hardships and dangers of their isolated mountain life, they had been given the gift of a relatively untroubled childhood. For the first time in their lives they could truly be carefree children, running and playing – and learning. Never had I witnessed such an outpouring of laughter and joy.

Apart from a set of monkey bars, a teeter-totter and a couple of basketball hoops, there seemed to be no playground equipment and the children were largely making up their own games. Some kids played with raggedy balls, while others kicked around a ball of tape. We made our way to Shirley's office, passing signs that read, "Children should be seen, heard, and believed," and "Speak your mind, even if your voice shakes."

As we watched, an elegantly dressed woman no taller than the Himalayan mountain women we had met in the villages approached. Shirley turned out to have grown up in Canada. She had first encountered Thrangu Rinpoche in Victoria (small world!), and then followed him to Nepal for his annual teachings, where she visited his school and eventually decided to devote herself to it. She is tiny in stature, but it quickly became apparent she is large in spirit and a force to be reckoned with. She has the heart of an angel, the gentle smile of a child and the eyes of a dragon. She also has the energy of someone decades younger. For over 20 years, Shirley has devoted herself to the SMD school. And while she is the director of the school, and charged with a vast number of complicated and demanding administrative duties, to the more than 500 kids at SMD she is a mentor and a mother. She is their champion. She loves them with everything she has, and they love her back with boundless affection. She has given her life to them.

Shirley was happy to finally meet us in person and eager to shed more light on the school, which admits children in "nursery" as early as 4 years old. In addition to the regular Nepali government curriculum of math, science, social studies, computer science, English and Nepali classes, the students also learn the Tibetan language, Dharma and meditation. Shirley was particularly eager to tell us about the children and the challenges involved in preparing them for their new lives. When they first arrive at the school from their mountain villages, usually after gruelling treks that last for days or even weeks, most suffer from severe malnutrition, and many have parasites or viral infections or other medical issues that must be dealt with. They are also coming into an environment that is radically different from anything most of them have ever been exposed to, which causes its own problems. Yet, despite being separated from their families for the first time in their lives, and living so far away from home in such a different world, the children generally adapt well, she said. At first, they may go through a state of withdrawal, but after a few weeks they adjust to their new life, and their school peers become their second family.

Shirley mused on how unprecedented it was for Thrangu Rinpoche to have decided to admit Karma without her having to go through any of the usual application procedures. "He's never done that before," she told us. She speculated that his decision had something to do with the fact that he has an acute ability to see the past, present and future at once, so perhaps he had seen something auspicious in the intricate connections that bound us to Karma. Or perhaps what had happened was related to the Buddhist belief that, when something is pursued with selflessness, all barriers will fall away.

Soon one of the senior students brought Karma up to Shirley's office to see us. She was indeed "full of beans," as Shirley had described her. Even though a year had gone by since we last saw each other, which is an eternity in the life of a child that young, Karma was thrilled to be reunited with us. We embraced as though no time had passed, and Karma's dimpled smile, which we knew so well, reappeared at once. As it was time for lunch, Karma ate with us in Shirley's office – lentils on rice with some cooked vegetables. The meal was typical of what the kids ate nearly every day. Once in a while they might receive an egg as a treat, but never any meat because the school is Buddhist, and in any case meat is expensive. A slice of apple was served for dessert. Apparently, the children considered the apple a treat. It was probably the only fruit they would be given.

Because it was the first day of school, classes wouldn't start until later that afternoon. So after lunch we had time to tour the school with Shirley and Karma. We met the school's medic, Wangchuk, who, due to staff shortages, had also assumed some of the school's vice-principal duties that year. He had his hands full doing intake for some hundred new students, only three of whom had sponsors, Karma being one of them.

We then visited the meal hall, where over 500 kids were eating their lunch; the shrine hall, which was a large open hall with a statue of Buddha at the front where the children practised the Dharma; the school library, consisting of a few bookshelves lining the walls of an otherwise empty room; and the computer lab, where there were about ten older desktop computers, which had to serve the entire school.

Next we saw the dorm rooms, which were located in two block-long concrete buildings, one for the boys and the other for the girls. Each of the rooms slept from four to 16 kids in rickety, steel-frame bunk beds, some stacked three high. None of the rooms had electricity or heating, and with the exception of the occasional stuffed animal or magazine page posted up here and there, the rooms seemed devoid of decoration or personal possessions. We found it hard to imagine how unpleasant life here must be when the kids had to remain indoors during the months-long winter and monsoon seasons.

Of course, no matter what hardships the children faced at SMD, we knew the school offered them their best chance at a future. They would get a good secular education while furthering their studies of the Dharma and their culture, and would escape the fate of those left behind in the villages. Once they'd reached the age of 6 or 7, the age Karma was when we met her, most of the village children would begin to work long hours – tending to the cattle, farming and planting, collecting cow dung and firewood for cooking, and washing clothes, all while also helping to take care of their siblings and the household. If they didn't die young of some easily treatable disease, many would go on to marry by the age of 14 or 15, and they'd soon have children of their own.

Soon it was time for class, so we walked Karma to her classroom – thrilled to be able to share that first momentous day in her new life with her. Peering in from the entrance, we saw three large wooden tables that occupied most of the space, with about 20 children sitting cross-legged on the floor around the tables. Most of the children were around Karma's age or younger, some of them wearing the maroon robes that signified they had been consigned to the monastery as monks or nuns. For many families, that was the only way they could ensure their children received a decent education and three nutritious meals a day. The other children wore the crisp white uniforms of SMD, fashioned in the traditional Tibetan style with a single stripe of colour down one side. A stack of books was presented to each child. We watched as Karma, unable to contain her excitement, began to leaf through her books at once, as though she'd been given a boatload of knowledge she had to try to soak up as fast as possible.

Until that moment it had not fully dawned on me how privileged the children of Canada are – indeed, the children of any country that is not in the Third World. Even most of the children who grow up poor in Canada, for example, would have access to books, to a library, to knowledge. And for any child of the middle or upper class, the world is truly their oyster. They can go to museums, take in exciting sports events, attend concerts and plays and dance performances of all kinds. They can even act or dance or play in one if they so choose. They can travel freely within their country, or to others. They can see different places, different cultures and all kinds of wonders of the world. Even if they can't physically go there, they can experience just about anything by way of the internet, to which virtually all of them have access.

Before we left our hotel, the front desk manager had asked me what brought us to Boudha. When I told her about Karma, the young woman's eyes began tearing up. "Thank you, sir, for allowing this young girl to dream bigger."

Now I understood why she had been so moved. We in the West remain ignorant of how fortunate we are. Our children are taught to dream as big as they want. That anything can be accomplished. But that young woman at the hotel knew all this. Perhaps she knew it from personal experience, or perhaps she was just aware of the extraordinary challenges faced by children of the Third World.

Up until now, a five-kilometre radius around her village had bound Karma's world. There was no TV, no internet, no phone, no electricity and only monastery scriptures and a handful of raggedy old books in the entire village. All Karma knew of the outside world came to her from the stories and pictures brought back from villagers who may have travelled down to Kathmandu, and the odd glimpse of foreigners passing through with our high-tech clothes and fancy smartphones.

I don't know how Karma imagined her future when she was living in Nar. But now, by virtue of the stack of books that had been placed before her, Karma's world, and her dreams, had just become a little bit bigger.

NINETEEN

According to Buddhism, there are three types of giving: giving, great giving and difficult giving. Difficult giving means to give of ourselves: our body, our mind, our life.

As legend has it, many years ago the three sons of a great king went hunting together in the jungle. On their journey, they came across a starving tigress in a cave. She was so weak she couldn't move, and she used what little remaining strength she had to protect her cubs. The youngest of the princes, who was known for his great compassion and generosity, told his brothers to go ahead. Unwilling to abandon the starving tigress, he chose to stay behind, but then he found himself in a dilemma. If he killed another animal to save the tigress, he would be taking a life to save a life. If he left the tigress, her cubs would surely die. His only option was to give in a way he had never done. He would give his own life to the tigress, so she might live on with her cubs.

Some time later, when the young prince did not return, his parents and brothers began to search for him. When they returned to the cave where he had last been seen, all they found were the remnants of his bones. They were crushed by his death and mourned him at length. The young prince's spirit returned and spoke to his family: "Please do not be unhappy. The end of birth is disintegration, and the end of gathering is separation. No one can transcend this for it is the nature of things. It is the same for everyone. If you perform evil actions, you will fall into the hell realms. If you perform virtuous actions, you will be reborn into higher realms. Therefore, diligently pursue virtue, and in the next life we will meet again."[12]

Inspired by their son, his family constructed a stupa around his bones, and they lived out the rest of their days pursuing only virtuous acts so they might eventually reunite with him. To this day, the story of the prince – believed to be a reincarnation of Buddha himself – is recounted, and the place where he sacrificed himself to the tigress – called Namo Buddha – has become a pilgrimage site for Buddhists from around the world. Namo Buddha is one of the three most important such sites in Nepal, along with the Boudha Stupa and the Swayambhunath Stupa.[13] It is also the site of the Thrangu Tashi Yangtse Monastery, founded by the same Tibetan lama who founded Karma's school – Thrangu Rinpoche. Since it is only about 40 kilometres from Karma's school in Boudha, Chantal and I decided to pay the monastery a visit.

The gravel road we took to Namo Buddha ended at the top of a mountain. White clouds floated across the sky, their shadows brushing verdant green hills that extended as far as the eye could see before disappearing into the snow-capped Himalayan peaks on the horizon. The lush rich smells of nature, a chorus of singing, chattering jungle birds – and an almost instant sense of peace and reverence – greeted us.

Rinpoche's monastery bore a striking resemblance to the one we visited back home in Canada, with the same red brick walls, intricately crafted detail and golden, pagoda-like roofs. It differed only in that it was much larger and was built into the side of the hilltop. The head administrator monk at Rinpoche's monastery in Canada had told us to look for KP, and to mention his name. It didn't take long for us to find KP. He seemed to be a high-ranking monk who had managerial duties at the monastery. He was stout and stood firmly upon the earth, yet his spirit was light and youthful. Thick glasses framed his nose, and he wore the same simple burgundy robe we had seen on hundreds of other monks.

For some reason, I felt an almost familial connection with these monks. Perhaps it was that we shared the same heartfelt laugh and thirst for life. Or perhaps it was my keen interest in learning as much as possible from them. Whatever the reason, I couldn't get enough of them and was grateful for every opportunity to speak with them. Their devotion to Buddhism, their practice of kindness and compassion and their exploration of the inner self resonated deeply with me and inspired me.

Chantal, KP and I strolled the grounds of Namo Buddha under trees blown into twisted shapes by the high winds at this elevation, and then along the narrowing, ascending ridgeline trail. KP spoke about many topics – about life and death, and how they are two sides of the same phenomenon, not so distant from each other as we like to think. We continued up the ridgeline, pausing for a moment before a cave – one thought to be similar to the tigress's cave, where she had nearly died of starvation, and where the young prince had given his life to save her. As we approached the end of the ridge, and the highest point on the mountain, hundreds of strings of prayer flags coalesced from every direction into one giant spindle. We watched in silence as the wind rippled through thousands of the brilliantly coloured flags, setting them aflutter against a crystal blue sky.

"What does it mean to be Buddhist?" I asked my red-robed companion.

KP's gaze moved outward toward the hills beyond the prayer flags. "People often think of Buddhism as a religion. But that is only one pillar of Buddhism. Buddhism has two more pillars. It is a science, and it is a philosophy of life." KP turned his back to the flags and we began our slow descent to the monastery. "Because I wear a robe, does that make me Buddhist?"

I thought about his question for a moment, not knowing if this was some sort of trick question. But the stout monk continued. "For example, if you and I exchanged clothes, and you were the one wearing my robe, and I your jeans and T-shirt, would that really change who we are?"

"No. It wouldn't."

"Yet because I wear a robe, people believe I am Buddhist, and come to me seeking answers they believe a Buddhist monk should give. But that is their view of who I am. It does not mean it is my view of who I am. Buddhism is about practising acceptance, and kindness. It is about practising love and compassion. Each of us has the ability to practise these things, in every act, and in every area of our lives, no matter where we are, no matter who we are. That, in a sense, is what it means to be Buddhist. Now, come dine with us."

Chantal and I returned to the monastery with KP, where we were invited into a large dining hall. Sitting cross-legged on a wooden bench at the back of the room, we listened to over a hundred monks chant their prayers before their meal. Their echoing voices filled every corner of the dining hall, the sound travelling through the open windows and beyond. And then, with hearty plates of rice and curried potatoes, we feasted together.

Following lunch, as we were about to leave, KP brought over another monk whom he introduced as Lama Tashi. The young lama was looking to travel down to Boudha. Since we were headed in that direction, we offered him a ride. I was secretly thrilled, as it would take us nearly two hours to get there travelling on the rough and potholed roads, and I would have him all to myself for that time, to ask as many questions as I could think of.

For the several hours we spent together, Lama Tashi and I conversed without a break. My questions must have flapped at him like an unruly string of prayer flags. We spoke about many things that day. Lama Tashi explained to me about the Buddhist Wheel of Life, elaborating on what Dawa had started to explain to me back in Phu.

He explained how each of us is continually reincarnated into different realms, and how, with every incarnation, we face different types of suffering. These sufferings are meant to teach us, so we may grow in wisdom and compassion over many, many lifetimes and eventually free ourselves of the cycle of birth and rebirth, known as samsara. There are six realms, and each realm is represented by one of the six syllables of the mantra, "om mani padme hum." The lower half of the Wheel of Life includes the animal and the hungry ghost realms. Beings in the animal realm suffer from ignorance and stupidity. Those in the hungry ghost realm will always be starving – ever hollow in their insatiable desire for more. Those at the very bottom of the wheel exist in the realm of hell, where everyone is perpetually angry and hateful. The upper half of the wheel includes the realms of the demigods, the gods and the humans. The demigods suffer from jealousy and envy, always competing with each other and with the gods. The gods are proud, powerful beings that live well but are indifferent to the sufferings of others, lacking in compassion. Though they enjoy their lives, at the moment before death, the gods suffer greatly, realizing for a fragment of a second how their pride has blinded them and consigned them to falling into one of the lower realms in their next reincarnation. The human realm, though not the highest, is the only realm from which beings may eventually escape samsara. But most humans are too blinded by desire and passion, and wrapped up in materialistic pursuits, to achieve enlightenment.

Our journey with Lama Tashi took us to the Durbar Square of Bhaktapur, a great plaza before the Royal Palace of the old Bhaktapur kingdom. Home to royalty until 1769, the palace and its many adjacent temples and artworks are now a tourist attraction and UNESCO World Heritage Site. We strolled among the intricately carved sculptures and pagodas, masterpieces crafted during the 17th and 18th centuries by ancient techniques long since forgotten.

I still had more questions for Lama Tashi. Reflecting on my passion for climbing mountains, I asked, "What if I continue to want to climb – not for the greed of praise or recognition, or to satisfy the ego of attaining a summit, but simply because of the personal journey it creates?"

"Having ambition and dreaming big is good, as long as you are always completely satisfied with living with very little."

I couldn't stop thinking about what Lama Tashi had said about the Wheel of Life. "How is it decided which realm we enter – what can we do to be free of the cycle?"

"Our actions from our previous lives will dictate which realm we enter next. It is our karma. You can understand your past by looking at your present life. To understand your future, look at your present choices. Reincarnating into the realms enables us to achieve enlightenment – only then can we be outside the cycle."

"How do you define enlightenment?"

The young lama paused for a moment. "It is freedom of view."

"Freedom of view?"

"Yes. We each have a different view. Having a different view creates suffering. Look at that wooden chair. We would all agree it is a wooden chair. Yet each of us will have a different view of it, depending on the way we each look at it. Once we can free ourselves of our own unique view, and see it first for what it is, a chair, then we have achieved freedom of view. It is the same when we look at a fancy meal or a simple meal, or a big bed or a small bed, or a rich person or a beggar – once we can truly see them as what they are, simply a meal, a bed or a human being, nothing more, nothing less, that is when we have achieved freedom of view."

"And how would you say we can practise achieving that?"

"We achieve it by practising compassion and kindness. The more we practise this, the more we free ourselves from our own mind, from our own prejudices, and from our own view."

At last it came time for us to part, and Lama Tashi drifted quietly away from us. I watched as his maroon robe receded into the distance until it became one of the myriad colours in the swirling crowd. And then the young lama was gone.

TWENTY

I'll never forget the look of wonder and excitement in her eyes. Her dimpled smiles and carefree laughter. The way she looked at her new teachers, in admiration and even awe. How other children flocked around her, calling after her, "Karma! Karma!" – attracted by her bright aura and passion for life. As Chantal and I spent time with Karma during her first days at SMD, I witnessed a girl who was not afraid of her new surroundings. She embraced this huge change in her life not just with courage but with excitement – every chance she had, she fiercely leafed through her books, scanning the images and text faster than she could grasp them. Her favourite subject, as we had asked her back in Nar, was still English. She found it the most interesting, she would say. Chantal and I supposed that perhaps it was because she associated English with learning about the world. And she interacted with her new environment, as if the whole world had just opened up to her and she was thrilled to be taking it all in.

Only too soon, our ten-day visit with Karma neared its end. Before we flew back to Canada, Chantal and I wanted to do something special for her – something that would show her more of the world around her, give her a new experience we could share as a family. We thought about taking her to the temples and the museums and the historical sites around Kathmandu, but the city seemed as though it would be overwhelming to her, and it was not a very kid-friendly place. So we ended up asking the senior students at SMD what they would have liked at Karma's age.

"The zoo!" was the consensus among the SMD seniors, who seemed to feel this was an answer so obvious they couldn't believe we had to ask.

Neither Chantal nor I was particularly fond of zoos, and we were also concerned about what conditions would be like at the Kathmandu zoo. Given that Nepal was one of the poorest countries in Asia, and we'd seen plenty of people on the streets that were visibly hungry and ill, we were afraid the zoo animals would also be suffering, which would surely be upsetting for Karma to see. Nevertheless, since everyone we asked agreed it would be a tremendous experience for her, we thought we'd give it a go.

To our surprise, Nepal's Central Zoo was well kept, much better than we had feared. In fact, the animals seemed to enjoy better living conditions than many of Kathmandu's most impoverished citizens. The zoo was home to about 870 exotic animals, including an assortment of endangered species, among them the great Royal Bengal tiger.

We toured the grounds with Karma and her older sister Nyima, a nun, who had joined us for the day. Nyima had the same gentle eyes and heartfelt smile as Karma, and she seemed glad to be able to spend time with Karma and us at the zoo. It was evident she loved Karma very much, and that she was happy to be reunited with her little sister, seeing her so full of life. The abbey where Nyima lived, which was in Swayambhunath on the outskirts of Kathmandu – where we had visited the so-called Monkey Temple on our first visit to Nepal – was another of Thrangu Rinpoche's institutions. Nyima was 18 years old at the time, and her English was good enough for communicating with us, and for doing much of the translating with Karma. As soon as we entered the gates, Karma was so excited she began racing around the zoo from one enclosure to the next, tugging at our hands, trying to soak in as much as she possibly could, all the while chattering away in Nepali, or perhaps in Narpa, her own language – we couldn't tell the difference. She lobbed such a rapid-fire volley of questions at her sister that Nyima couldn't translate fast enough.

"Why do the animals have tags in their ears?" "Why do some have horns and others do not?" "How did they get the tiger into the cage?" "How come that man took the money from the elephant?" (Visitors could pet the elephant if they gave it money, which it would very carefully take with its trunk and pass off to the mahout.) And when she wasn't asking questions, or staring with wonder at the animals, she was doing imitations of their sounds.

In the middle of the zoo, we came upon a swing set. It was a standard A-framed set, with chipping paint and a metal seat suspended by chains from the bar above. But for Karma, who had never seen one before, let alone ridden one, it was nothing short of amazing. Karma hopped onto the seat, and when Chantal began to push her, she pumped her legs to pick up speed until, her eyes wide with wonder, she flew freely through the air with the wind streaming through her long dark hair.

Karma was captivated by many of the creatures that day, but of them all she loved the birds the most. The parakeets and their wild calls, the funny-looking cockatoo with its yellow mohawk, the toucans with their strangely large beaks, the light, graceful motions of the macaws, the vibrant colours – they thrilled and delighted her. And when a large male peacock fanned its bright tail feathers, opening them into a stunning half-circle of greens and blues, Karma was mesmerized.

After the animals came the amusement park, which consisted of exactly two rides: a rather tame-looking roller coaster for children, and a much scarier one called the Funny Temple – a handful of bucket seats attached to a large saucer that spun in circles, revolving forward then backward, dropping down and climbing up again. Karma stared intently at the Funny Temple, her eyes lit up in eager anticipation. Chantal and I looked at each other, uncertain about whether we should let her go, and then at Nyima, who said it was up to Karma, and then at Karma, asking her if she was sure she didn't want to go on the kids' roller coaster instead? Karma wrinkled her nose. No, she did not. Pointing to the Funny Temple, she made it clear what she wanted most was to ride that spinning saucer in the sky. So Karma and I climbed into one of the metal buckets, and the rusty machine started up with a grinding sound and began to move to its own rhythm – slow at first, and then faster and faster, until we were whirling so fast above the crowds I feared the thing would take off. Round and round we flew, catching the occasional half-second glimpse of Chantal as she cheered us on before we were whipped away again. All the while Karma was grinning ear to ear with exhilaration and erupting in giggles, while I, jaw clamped in a forced smile, tried as best I could not to think about the last time the machine had been serviced.

There were many, many firsts for Karma that day: her first time in a car; first time eating in a restaurant; first time in a boat; first time on a swing; first time on an amusement park ride; first time seeing a royal palace; and, of course, first time at a zoo, seeing a tremendous variety of animals, including rhinoceros, a tiger, an elephant, a hippopotamus, antelope and deer, reptiles and hundreds of species of birds and fish.

I thought about our friends back home in Canada and how they often commended us on the "good things" we were doing for this little girl. But, truth be told, what we did for her paled in comparison to what she was doing for us. Being able to witness these moments in her life, the simple joy she took in each and every new experience and the immense gratitude she felt for them was a gift far greater than any we gave to her. Neither Chantal nor I had ever felt a burning desire to have children. But now we had Karma in our lives and we felt deeply fulfilled.

Before exiting the park that day, we walked past the merchant stands that were selling everything from ice cream cones to cotton candy, cheap plastic animal toys, oversized stuffed animals and Mylar balloons. Packs of kids flocked from one stand to the next, pleading with their parents to buy them stuff. We kept walking and Karma kept moving alongside us, paying little attention to it all. I wondered why she seemed so indifferent to the stuff the other kids wanted so badly. And then wondered if there was, in fact, anything she did want.

"Nyima, could you please ask Karma if she needs anything?"

Karma shook her head no.

"Does she need anything whatsoever, for school or for her room?"

Karma shook her head once more.

"We're going back to Canada tomorrow. If there is something she needs, please let us know."

Karma spoke quietly in her native language. Nyima translated.

"She would really like a pair of closed shoes."

"Closed shoes? Like runners?"

"Yes."

"Of course, we will get her a pair of closed shoes." My mind suddenly turned to the trek from her village.

"Nyima, what did Karma wear to hike down from the mountains?"

"Her Crocs."

An 8-year-old girl, leaving her entire world behind, trekking into the unknown, for five days through the high Himalaya. Through the wind, rain, mud and snow. Over rock and ice, across freezing rivers and along dangerously narrow craggy cliff sides. All in her imitation Crocs.

The next morning, Chantal and I visited the school one more time to say goodbye to Karma. It wasn't easy for the three of us to communicate with each other, but even when there wasn't a translator around, Chantal, Karma and I found our own ways to say what we needed to – through the expressions on our faces, hand gestures, body language and the occasional English or Nepali word. When we somehow managed to explain to Karma that today was our last day and we were leaving for home in a few hours, Karma's head dropped to her chest and tears sprang to her eyes. She grasped both of our hands, holding on tight. Never had I said a goodbye that heart-wrenching. Tears escaped Chantal's eyes, and I fought with every ounce of strength to hold my own back.

Karma looked as though she really wanted to ask us something but couldn't get the words out. In her Tibetan Buddhist culture, it's not polite to ask for anything. Chantal and I each gave her a heart-to-heart hug and then, sensing this was what she wanted to know, we told her we would be back soon. She seemed to understand because her tears stopped and the bright smile we had come to know so well reappeared on her shining face.

TWENTY-ONE

The path through the labyrinth around the grand Boudhanath Stupa was slowly beginning to reveal itself to us. Where once we had found the unmarked alleys and maze-like passages winding every which way around the stupa all but impenetrable, on this second visit to see Karma we felt almost like locals, able to weave ourselves seamlessly into the constant flow of movement around us. And the movement certainly was ceaseless.

The narrow streets were overrun with motorbikes, bicycles and cars. Packed into every remaining open space were the people – the locals, the street vendors, the tourists, the pleading beggars, the monks and nuns. Yet now that we were familiar with Boudha, Chantal and I travelled at the same brisk pace we were accustomed to when commuting along one of Vancouver's downtown walkways. Skipping up and down the sidewalks to avoid obstacles, dodging cars and motorbikes, hopping over piles of feces covered with flies and potholes deep enough to twist an ankle, we forged ahead. We were on a mission – to get to SMD as fast as possible. It was April 2014, and Chantal and I were back in Nepal, a full year since spending those few precious days with Karma when she first arrived at SMD. Although we had written letters to each other throughout the year, Chantal and I missed Karma deeply and couldn't wait to see her again.

Under the searing heat of the day I could feel the sweat on my back starting to seep through my shirt against the weight of my 60-litre backpack. Usually it would be packed full of climbing gear, but this time it was stuffed with dozens of bottles of children's multivitamins. My sister, a naturopathic doctor, had been able to get the vitamins partially sponsored, and with the help of other family and friends, Chantal and I had paid the remaining costs. Shirley had told us that high-quality multivitamins were hard to find and very expensive in Nepal, but so many of the kids at her school arrived suffering from severe malnutrition that we wanted to do something to help. Since shipping them was cost-prohibitive, considering both the freight and duties that would have to be paid, the best way to bring them was through visitors to the school – like ourselves. Although the 3,000 some odd tablets we were bringing might have seemed like a lot, they were hardly enough to make a small dent for the over 500 children at SMD. But out here in Kathmandu, every bit counted.

After a few more twists and turns, we arrived at the large green steel gates of SMD. The new school year had not yet begun, and the school-yard was filled with hundreds of children, running to and fro. All around us echoed the sounds of laughter and play. Within minutes, out of the mix, a familiar face approached. She was a touch taller, and her hair, which had earlier been thin and with something of the reddish cast typical of the malnourished, had grown in thick and was several shades darker. Her smile was as bright as when we'd last seen her, her large brown eyes still beaming and her embrace as spirited as the day we first met. It had been a year since we'd seen Karma, two years since we'd seen her teaching that class in Nar. But the way the three of us felt when we saw each other again, it was as though no time had passed.

Behind Karma, I caught the soft, frightened eyes of a small figure peering out at us. She looked lost. Chantal saw her too, and in a moment we both recognized her. She was little Pemba, Karma's youngest sister, whom we had met in their home in Nar. Back then, she was a 3-year-old toddler, running around Karma's home and hijacking the conversations. Now, at 5 years old, she was a little girl, curious but shy, hiding behind her sister. I didn't know if she remembered us, but Chantal and I embraced her nonetheless. In that moment, the three of us became four.

We then learned that their cousin, Dawa Tashi, the monk, had managed to gain Thrangu Rinpoche's ear. Thanks to him, and also to Karma's outstanding performance at school (Karma was eager to show us her first-year report card, which was almost straight As), little Pemba had been able to gain admission to SMD as well. We also learned, much to our surprise, that Karma and Pemba's father, Sonam, whom we had never met, had made the long journey down from Nar to bring Pemba to the school and that it was literally just moments before we arrived that he'd dropped her off. No wonder she looked like someone lost, someone who had left everything familiar behind her. That's exactly who she was.

We had missed Sonam by a hair. One of the senior students, Dorje, helped us call Sonam, who had now joined the ever-growing numbers of people in Nepal, even those in the remotest areas, who had cellphones. He was already en route to his room near the abbey at Swayambhunath, on the other side of town, where his daughters Nyima and Wangyal lived. But when he learned we had arrived at the school, he began to make his way back through the Kathmandu mayhem at once.

The minute I saw Sonam, I recognized him. Not because of a physical resemblance to Karma or Pemba, but because he had the same glow about him as they did. Strangely, I felt the same connection to him – something familial, as though we had known each other for many years. Like many of the other mountain dwellers we had come to know, Sonam was short but stout. He scarcely reached my neckline, yet his large spirit commanded the space around him. He moved lightly, almost like a feather, and radiated kindness. He had the same gentle eyes and bright smile as his girls.

Sonam approached me, his eyes never leaving mine, his smile never wavering. We grasped each other's hands firmly and spoke to each other without speaking. Sonam couldn't speak a word of English, but Dorje, the senior SMD student we had just met, was happy to translate. It turned out Dorje was also from Nar, and their families knew each other well. The first words Sonam spoke to me were an apology for not having learned enough English to be able to speak to me. This nearly floored me. We, after all, were in Nepal and had learned almost no Nepalese.

That evening Chantal and I took Sonam, Karma and Dorje to a nearby restaurant called the Garden Kitchen. As it was after 6:00 p.m., and soon to be pitch dark in Kathmandu, it was thought to be too late to take Pemba with us, so she stayed at the school while the rest of us went out. Though it might have seemed strange to leave behind a child who had literally just arrived, that is how things are done at SMD. Families from remote mountain villages don't have the luxury of staying weeks or days or even hours with their children to acclimate them to their new environment. The children are dropped off, and although it's a shock at first, they are soon absorbed into the school.

Walking down the winding passages of Boudha at night was a very different experience than in daylight. The commotion had not died down, and the streets were as full as ever, but with hardly any street lamps, everything was dark. Faces were hidden in shadows, and stray dogs, asleep during the day, now roamed and scavenged the narrow pathways. Though Sonam had been to Kathmandu before, it was clear he wasn't comfortable being out in it at night. Everything he had brought with him was in a small backpack, which he held onto tightly. Never did he let go of the backpack – not even while we were in the restaurant. Karma, too, felt uncomfortable being out in the streets after dark. She had been at SMD for a year, but had never really gone beyond the confines of the school, especially at night. She stayed close to Chantal, holding onto her arm, always cautiously on the lookout, quick to startle even at the sound of a dog bark.

The Garden Kitchen Restaurant, which catered to monks and tourists alike, was a little oasis of peace in the middle of Boudhanath. With its outdoor courtyard neatly planted with shrubs and trees, its comfortable indoor cafe-like lounge and an assortment of artisanal teas and local arts and crafts for sale, it reminded me a bit of the small cafes I was used to back home.

We shared many things with Sonam that evening. Chantal and I told him about our first encounter with Karma back in Nar, how she had bonded with Chantal while dancing and how Karma had approached us to learn English. We told him about meeting Thrangu Rinpoche in Canada, and that he had a monastery not far from our home. Sonam seemed to like this very much. Sonam, in turn, filled us in on some of their family life. He explained that he and Pema had two sons before Karma, who both died in infancy. Infant mortality, we had learned, was high in the mountain villages, with many children dying from common childhood diseases or malnutrition. In many of the mountain villages, three out of four children die before reaching their fifth birthday. Sonam went on to tell us about Karma's birth. When the villagers learned that the child who arrived after the deaths of their two male children was a girl – the fifth girl born to Sonam and Pema, with no surviving boys – they told Sonam and his family this was a bad omen. However, when the umbilical cord attached to Karma fell away without being cut, suddenly the villagers reversed themselves. They grew excited, exclaiming this was a very good omen, and that Karma would bring much fortune to their family. I wondered if this was why they had chosen the name Karma for her.

Sonam told us about Palma, his middle daughter, who was studying in a remote school near Pokhara. He also shared with us his feeling that the most important thing was that his girls never forget where they're from, and that they never forget their Dharma, their way of being. Chantal and I wholeheartedly agreed with this. That was why we had felt SMD was so right for Karma.

Before dinner was over, we asked Sonam's permission to take Karma to Chitwan National Park, a Nepalese animal sanctuary that is home to 68 species of mammals. Karma had been so excited by the animals she'd seen at the zoo the previous year that Chantal and I figured she would be thrilled to see animals in their natural habitat. We also thought this would be a great opportunity for her to see another part of her country, to experience the jungles and varied landscapes of the Terai lowlands in the far south of Nepal. We would go for a few days before classes began. Before we'd known that Sonam was going to be in Kathmandu we had asked permission of Karma's older sister Nyima, who was acting as her guardian in the absence of her parents. But now that Sonam was here, we wanted to make sure it was okay with him, and he gladly agreed.

We each had so many questions for each other; so much to share, so much to learn. With all this animated conversation, young Dorje doing his best to translate back and forth, the evening passed quickly. Only too soon it was time for us to depart and go our separate ways. Before he left, Sonam knelt down next to Karma. Locking his bright eyes onto hers, he spoke gently to her, smiling all the time, though I'm sure saying goodbye to her must have been very hard for him. And then, after another handshake, we insisted on putting Sonam into a taxi back to his room, so he wouldn't have to make his way through the dark, winding streets on foot. He seemed both very relieved and grateful.

The next day Sonam would travel north, returning to his home in the mountains, and we would travel south with Karma. We didn't know when we'd see Sonam again, nor did he know when he would next see Karma or Pemba. Maybe a year, maybe years. But for us the most important thing was that there was now a genuine and deeply felt bond with Sonam – one that would not diminish over distance or time. We were now connected through our mutual love for Karma and Pemba, but also through affection and respect for each other. We had become family.

TWENTY-TWO

Saturday, April 25, 2015, began as a normal spring morning for Chantal and me, back in Vancouver. For the Nepalese, however, as we were about to learn, it was a day that left them reeling from the most devastating earthquake they had witnessed in recent history. During the early afternoon, which was the middle of our night, tectonic plates spanning the length of the Himalaya abruptly compressed and fractured, causing a 7.8 magnitude earthquake that struck near Kathmandu and its neighbouring valleys. By the time Chantal and I woke up, thousands of people were reported dead, and tens of thousands were missing. Early images began to flood the internet, revealing the extent of the destruction around Kathmandu. Brick buildings were reduced to unrecognizable piles of rubble, as though convoys of tanks had bulldozed through the city. Dust-covered corpses lay partially buried amid the debris. Cracks wide enough to swallow entire vehicles split the streets apart. Many of Nepal's most sacred structures, including the intricately crafted, timeless temples and pagodas in Bhaktapur we had walked among with Lama Tashi two years before, were now flattened heaps of debris. Temples in Patan dating back to the third century, where we had lunch with Karma after our visit to the zoo, were levelled. The great tower of Dharahara, a nearly two-centuries-old watchtower said to have been built for a queen, and a UNESCO heritage site, was a pile of rock. The force of the quake reached the great Boudha Stupa near Karma's school as well, perforating it with deep fissures that spread up the sacred monument like hollow fingers and toppled its central spire. The bodies of locals, as well as tourists, were already being pulled from the wreckage. Every few minutes brought news of hundreds more being added to the death toll.

Chantal and I stood in our kitchen in shock as the news flooded in. Over the previous three years, we had come to love Karma and Pemba as our own daughters. And now we had no way of telling whether they were alive. Whether they were hurt, alone or afraid. It was impossible to reach anyone by phone. Never had I felt so utterly helpless. Both of us tried to stay strong. Both of us kept breaking down. Our thoughts began to extend to all the people who had come to be so dear to us on our visits over the last few years, including Shirley. We thought about Karma's family – about Nyima and Wangyal, Karma's two nun sisters at the Thrangu Tara abbey near Swayambhunath, about Sonam, Pema and Lhakpa, in their house of clay and stone so far away from any aid or resources, and so near to the epicentre of the quake. We thought about SMD and the 500 children it housed, unaware if the school was even still standing. We thought about Nepal, one of Asia's poorest countries, already riddled with disease, garbage and extreme poverty – how would they cope with such rampant destruction?

And then Chantal turned to me. "Mike, we were supposed to be in Nepal now."

Chantal and I looked at each other in disbelief. She was right. We had been travelling to Nepal each April and had planned to be there again that month. However, at the time we were still in the middle of building a home for ourselves in a new place – a plan that had been seeded when we were in Phu back in 2012, when we'd decided we should move away from our fast-paced city life to a place where we could be closer to nature. Almost serendipitously, we had discovered a building lot in Squamish, about 45 minutes north of Vancouver, which is known as the outdoor recreation destination for Canada and one of my favourite places on Earth. The lot was surrounded by trees, mountains and creeks, and was about a ten-minute hike out the front door to some of the best rock climbing in the world. Our new house was supposed to have been finished by that April, but we'd encountered some "normal" delays in the construction process, which meant we had decided to delay our trip to Nepal to the fall.

After my initial feeling of relief at having dodged a bullet, I felt we should get on the first plane to Kathmandu and help in any way we could. But Chantal reined me in, and I quickly realized that would be irresponsible. In the present state of chaos, we were likely to be more of a burden than help. Besides which, the landlocked country has only one international airport, and we began hearing reports of the damage it had sustained, which was preventing planes from landing or taking off. An hour went by without any news of our loved ones. And then two, and then several more. They were the longest hours of my life. And then a Facebook status update from Shirley appeared: "All friends of smd pls notify all our kids overseas and everyone else that we are ok. Lots of damage. Some fatalities in the neighbourhood. We are sheltering neighbours. Food, water, meds going to be needed in the [Kathmandu] valley. Here too."

The SMD school had been badly damaged but was still standing, and somehow, miraculously, none of the children or staff were injured. Though it was wonderful news that none of our friends were hurt, we would later discover that many of them and their families would suffer great hardship, losing their houses and in some cases their livelihoods.

We were greatly relieved by the news that everyone had survived, but we still felt a deep sadness within our hearts. We knew that, for Nepal, it would be a long road to recovery. And it took well over a year for Nepal even to begin to mend from the physical and psychological shock of the disaster. It didn't help that for months after the quake there were hundreds of aftershocks, including a second earthquake measuring 7.3 in magnitude that struck on May 12, just 17 days after the initial quake. It was another devastating blow. The quakes affected over eight million people, with about 9,000 deaths reported, 22,000 injured and nearly 800,000 homes destroyed or badly damaged. On top of this, nearly one million children could no longer attend school.[14] Of every ten schools in the most heavily damaged areas, nine had been reduced to rubble. Over 24,000 classrooms – gone. Tent cities, filled with shanty lean-tos cobbled together with tarp and canvas, popped up and sprawled throughout the city to house people, some of whom would have to live there for the next two years.

The terrible devastation didn't stop in Kathmandu, but much of the help did. Remote villages were left to fend for themselves, as most of the government and foreign aid was concentrated around the urban areas of Nepal's capital. Many settlements in the Gorkha region, usually a one- to two-day walk (or more) from larger settlements, were among the hardest hit. Severed from the rest of Nepal by earthquake-triggered landslides, the villagers, many of whom lost their homes and suffered from broken bones and deep lacerations, were now on their own, with no access to health care or shelter. Perhaps the worst hit was the popular tourist destination of Langtang. From one moment to the next, this village had literally been wiped off the face of the earth by a giant slide, taking with it 176 inhabitants, 80 foreigners and 10 military personnel. One hundred of the bodies were never found.[15]

Mount Everest was also hit, leaving hundreds of climbers stranded high up on the mountain. An avalanche of rock and earth tore through base camp like explosive cannon balls and shrapnel, killing and injuring dozens of climbers and Sherpas alike.

Yet the Nepali people fought their way back. Standing on their own feet, with little help from the outside world or from their own government, they shared resources and did what they could for each other. The SMD school became a makeshift refuge for people in the community who lost their homes. The school was already overcapacity with its students, yet somehow it made it work, all while keeping the children safe and dealing with the issues of sanitation and disease. The children stepped up too, lending their hands wherever help was needed. Their main building, which housed the school's shrine hall, dining hall and most of the classrooms, was rendered unsafe to use. Since it wasn't safe to sleep indoors during the aftershocks, the school's courtyard was repurposed with large tarpaulins where the children slept for days following the quakes. Garages were converted into classrooms. Tin roofs were erected in front of the girls' dormitory, and the children ate their meals at benches and tables that were placed beneath them. The children would live like this for over a year.

Over the weeks that followed, Chantal and I sprang into action, raising funds and awareness for Nepal and SMD. Not knowing how long it would take Nepal to recover from the earthquakes, nor how Karma and Pemba's education would be affected, we wanted to obtain visitor visas for the girls so they would have the option of coming to Canada – perhaps with an eye to coming to study here eventually, if they liked it during their visit, but if nothing else just to give them a break from the misery of their lives following the earthquakes. Their parents were in favour of this plan.

However, in order to get visitors' visas, we would first have to get the girls passports. With all the chaos in Kathmandu, young Dorje, the senior student from SMD who had helped us translate our conversations with Sonam the previous year, ended up having to wait in line at the passport office for three days to save their spot. When it was finally their turn, Shirley brought the girls down to the passport office. As if they hadn't faced enough challenges, en route to the passport office little Pemba was grazed by a hit-and-run van. Shirley cursed and kicked the van as it sped away. Such was Kathmandu. Fortunately, the 7-year-old was able to shake off this incident without so much as shedding a tear, and they made it to the passport office in time. Once the girls had their passports, we could proceed with the visitor visa applications, which involved having their father make the long journey down to sign the documents. We sent in as strong an application as we could. We even arranged for Karma and Pemba to be accepted into a summer English school program for international children under 14 years old.

Not only was their application to visit Canada declined, but the barriers stacked against them were so enormous that it was clear it would be virtually impossible to make this happen. It was the first time I felt anger toward my own country. While we didn't want to give up on the visitor visas, it didn't make sense to reapply. For each application, Sonam would have to leave his herd and make the long trek down to Kathmandu to sign the papers in person, which was a huge inconvenience, especially for such a low-probability event. It was infuriating, especially given the immigration office's rationale for refusing the application: that Karma and Pemba had no prior experience of travelling overseas, and that their parents did not have the financial means to bring them back to Nepal. We had specifically stated we would take care of all their financial needs in Canada, and included proof of a return flight ticket to Nepal, but the answer was still no.

Less than two months after the quakes, monsoon season arrived in Kathmandu. Up to 375 millimetres of rain falls in the city over the months of June to August, transforming it, at even the best of times, into a mud-spattered mess, where raw sewage, muck and garbage coalesce into an ankle-high watery sludge that spews throughout the streets. The children at SMD pushed on. They went to their classes and ate their meals outside in the mud and rain. When a sewage main up the street from the school, damaged during the earthquakes and never fixed, burst open from the deluge and flooded the entire school with raw bacteria-infested sewage, the children, barefoot and drenched from head to toe, worked together, shouldering one bucket at a time to carry out the sewer water from their school. Many of them were unable to communicate with their families in their home villages, and were unaware of whether their parents and siblings were hurt or even alive, and yet they pushed on. They never stopped pushing on.

There was no time to worry. There was no time to complain, or to feel tired or sorry for themselves. They dealt with the blows, over and over and over again, until they were utterly spent. And then they did it again. They did it without anger or bitterness. They did it for themselves, and they did it for each other. For this is how they had always done it. This was the will and resilience of the Nepali people.

TWENTY-THREE

The three-limbed monkey hobbled gingerly above the streets, grasping bundles of wire with his hands and remaining foot as he balanced along the electrical line. With tired yet resolute eyes and patched fur, he limped his way forward. Amid the crumbling structures and heaps of bricks, this damaged, valiant creature was the perfect image of Nepal itself.

It was October 2015, and Chantal and I were back for our third visit to Nepal since going for the first time in 2012. Never did we imagine seeing this beloved country in such a state. Six months after the devastating earthquake, Nepal still had a very long way to go to recovery. Half-destroyed buildings clung precariously to their foundations, and remnants of structures no longer even recognizable were heaped throughout the city. Thousands of people still lived in tents amid the mud and the rubble. But perhaps the most noticeable difference we observed was the terrible fatigue we saw in people's faces. It was clear the last six months had pushed the Nepali people to their very limits.

To make matters worse, just as we arrived in Kathmandu, a blockade had been set up at the border with India, halting imports into landlocked Nepal. The blockade was related to political complications that arose when a draft of Nepal's first constitution was released. After years of negotiations, tension and protests, Nepal had finally moved forward with a constitution. But in a country comprising over 100 different ethnic and caste groups, there were obviously going to be people who felt their interests were not adequately represented. Several minority groups, including the Madhesis, launched violent street protests in the south, near the

Indian border, and clashed with the state police, swarming and killing several police officers.[16] Curfews were put in place and broken, the protests intensified and still more people were shot and killed. India complained the new constitution was unfair to the Madhesis, with whom India has close geographic and historical ties. Though the Indian government denied having any influence over the blockade, it was clear it at least sanctioned it, for it did nothing to avert the catastrophic fuel and humanitarian crisis that ensued. Since Nepal relied on India for the majority of its imports, the blockade left the country bereft of critical supplies such as fuel, food, medicines and vaccines at precisely the moment they were most needed.[17] UNICEF and the US embassy issued statements about the disaster, citing three million children who were at risk of death or disease due to the severe shortages.[18]

Kathmandu looked like something out of a film about the apocalypse. It was strange seeing the once bustling streets we had become accustomed to now largely empty. One exception was the vehicles that lined the streets as far as three kilometres away from gas stations. People slept in their cars for days, waiting with no assurance they would even get gas. A black market emerged selling fuel at hideously exorbitant prices.

Since Nepalis primarily cooked with kerosene, cooking fuel was exhausted in a matter of days, forcing millions of people to start cutting the country's already sparse forests to fuel their stoves.[19]

Like the rest of Kathmandu, the SMD school had suffered considerable damage from the earthquakes and the monsoon. Its buildings were split by deep cracks that spread like veins throughout the walls, piercing both cement and brick. Colourful murals looked as though sledgehammers had been taken to them. Support beams had to be held together with dozens of steel reinforcements. Sewage mains in the girls' dormitory had fractured, releasing a pungent stench in their living quarters. A mountain of cut block wood was piled in the school's courtyard as fuel for the school's kitchen.

The kids' classes and meals were still conducted outside under the tin roofs. Even though the school had raised the funds to begin repairs on the school buildings, the funds had to go through a cumbersome bureaucratic process that would take several more months before receiving government approval to actually use the funds.

Amid it all, Karma's bright smile shone through the darkness. As soon as she spotted us, she rushed toward us with open arms, with her little sister Pemba in tow. Pemba's hair, which had been thin and reddish the last time we saw her, had grown in thick and dark like Karma's. Three nutritious meals a day – mostly lentils, rice and vegetables – had made a difference. Despite surviving a year of destruction, Pemba's face glowed like a lotus flower, her eyes gentle and hopeful with optimism. We embraced those two beautiful girls, holding them close. We were together again at last.

One of the first orders of business was to go down to the street market to get Karma and Pemba new shoes. No material could stand up to the harsh monsoons and winters in Kathmandu, and the shoes they wore were practically rotting off their feet. We passed a fresh fruit stand, and Karma's and Pemba's eyes lit up, fixated on the bananas. Usually the only fruit they would get was a slice of apple, but with all the turmoil over the last few months, I wasn't sure if they'd had even that.

"I have two little princesses with me, and I'm in need of your two finest bananas!"

The fruit vendor carefully plucked two bananas from behind him, as though he were picking the finest roses, and knelt down next to the girls, handing them their fruit, which caused huge smiles to spread across their faces.

My heart ached to see that. After everything these two had been through, they could still take joy from the simplest of things – being presented with a banana, savouring every bite. Nothing in them seemed to feel the injustice of what they – and their country – were going through. That was something to learn from.

Seeing what it meant to Karma and Pemba to have had this little outing, Chantal and I were determined to do something else for the kids. All the kids. We could tell the last six months had taken a toll on them, for they seemed much more subdued than in previous years. We spoke to Shirley and to the school's principal, who suggested that a day in the park would be the best thing for the children. It had been five years since they had been taken on a field trip to the park. Although the school is a safe environment for the kids, it is a concrete walled compound in the middle of the city with no green space. The kids craved nature – to be able to run around in a place with grass and trees. The only problem was that it was a 45-minute drive to get to the nearest park, and as we were in the middle of a nationwide fuel crisis, getting any sort of transportation would be challenging at best. But we left it to the monks, and they performed miracles. Within a day they had organized 14 buses to chauffeur 500 children, along with the school staff and teachers, to Thankot Park the following morning. The children were so excited they couldn't sleep.

Since the road to the school had been obliterated during the earthquake and ensuing monsoon, and no vehicle could travel it, we had to walk for about 20 minutes to reach the buses. The kids held hands and, two by two, they exited the school gates. We snaked our way through the narrow streets, passing gaping sinkholes that were big enough to swallow entire cars. We passed devastated buildings and half-crumbled walls. We skipped around open sewage and decaying garbage, stray dogs and half-rotted goat heads. Yet the children were all smiles, and for the first time in many months the sound of hundreds of children's laughter and singing echoed through the streets of Kathmandu.

The monks had made arrangements for the children to spend the entire day in the park, with breakfast, lunch, afternoon snacks and dinner fully catered. The school's principal even brought cake to commemorate the occasion.

Following a bumpy bus ride, interrupted by two bathroom breaks (which consisted of girls and boys running amid ruins and squatting next to each other) and accompanied by the cacophony of the children belting out Nepali folk songs, we arrived at the outskirts of Kathmandu, and our destination. Thankot Park was nothing more than an enclosed green space of grass, a few trees and a small pond. For the children, however, it meant a chance to be children again. A chance to forget the trauma, the filth, the destruction and the hardship of their lives. As they exited the buses and charged through the park gates, they seemed to explode with months of pent-up energy. Never in my life had I seen such an abundance of children's joy. So pure, unobstructed and spontaneous.

And very rarely in my life have I had the opportunity to give a gift that gave so much pleasure. Not only did it allow the children to have a day of much-needed carefree play but it also acted as a direct injection into Nepal's local economy, providing employment and income to the bus drivers and conductors, the catering staff, the cooks and the local food markets. It turned out to be the best thing Chantal and I could have done to help at that time.

After the picnic, we went ahead with another plan we had made for Karma and Pemba, which we had cleared with their family even before we arrived in Nepal. We wanted to take them away from Kathmandu and all its devastation to Temple Tree, a little family resort in Pokhara. Nepal's second-largest city, Pokhara had somehow escaped the earthquake, and for the girls it would be a way for them to escape it too, and to be in a beautiful place, one they had never seen before, if only for a few days.

Located at the foot of the southern midlands of the mighty Annapurna ranges, Pokhara is surrounded by vast, lushly forested hills, and boasts a view to the north of some of Nepal's most impressive peaks. It also hugs the shores of Phewa Lake, one of Nepal's largest and most gorgeous lakes. During our time there, the girls were able to swim in the pool at the resort – a first for them – and go paddling on the lake – another first. They loved being in Pokhara from the very moment we set foot there.

Even more important, being in Pokhara was a chance for them to reunite with their father, who made the long trip down the mountains to be with them and their sister Palma, then about 13 years old, who was studying at a school nearby.

The day after our arrival, Sonam came in with Palma, whom we had never met. She had the gentle demeanour we'd come to know in everyone in that family, as well as the same kind eyes and bright spirit. We weren't sure how long it had been since Karma and Pemba had last seen Palma – perhaps years. But it was very moving to see the tenderness and care with which they approached each other. They weren't demonstrative in the way we are, but that didn't get in the way of expressing their love for each other, which was palpable.

Sonam was the joyful, lighthearted man I remembered from our previous meeting, and even sported a cap with a Canadian flag on it. Even though we didn't share a language, we were able just by observing and being together to learn a lot about our different ways of doing things during those precious days together. The Himalayan mountain dwellers tend to be much more reserved than we are. Where Chantal and I were always hugging the girls and holding hands with them when we were out walking, their own father didn't do that, but he didn't seem to mind that we did. We also tend to talk a lot during meals, while it's their custom to enjoy each other's company without speaking at the table. Despite our differences, there was a genuine comfort and delight in being with each other. Somehow our time together was easy and uncomplicated, and the longer we spent together, the more it felt like being with family.

Each day Sonam would teach Chantal and me a bit more Nepali, and each day we would teach Sonam a bit more English. He took great pleasure in observing us teach the girls about subjects such as math and geography, and we learned a lot by watching how he parented his children. Always gentle yet firm, he took every opportunity he could to teach them how to behave. He saw to it that they shared with one another, and that they paid attention to their surroundings. It was clear he was a very intelligent, caring and compassionate father. And even though he was geographically separated from his girls, unable to see them for months or even years at a time, they had one of the deepest family bonds I have ever seen.

On our last day in Pokhara, we visited the International Mountain Museum. The museum has an impressive display of information about the history of mountaineering in Nepal, and about the geology and ecology of the Himalaya. Karma and Pemba found the display of climbing gear fascinating – the ice axes, crampons, heavy-duty mountaineering boots, oxygen bottles and masks, the thick down suits that make the climbers look like Martians and all the other gear involved in scaling some of the world's highest peaks. They'd lived among those peaks since they were born but never had any idea what was involved in climbing them.

The museum also has displays devoted to the people who live in the high mountain villages – people like themselves, in other words. As we passed one of the dioramas depicting village life, Sonam brought out his flip phone and began taking photos of the scene. It was a replica of a stone and clay house, just like the ones we saw in Phu and Nar, complete with an authentic *mdong mo* (a Tibetan butter tea churn), a dung-fuelled stove and manikins dressed in traditional chubas. Sonam smiled at me and said, "My home."

Something turned over inside of me at those words. It was hard for me to imagine what it would be like for someone to see his own way of life enshrined in a museum setting as something exotic – and possibly endangered. As we left the diorama and continued to look at the various displays, I couldn't let go of this thought. I wondered what would happen to the semi-nomadic life that has sustained Sonam and his people for many generations, and to the village where they made their home. Once their children are educated and exposed to the outside world and its opportunities, will they leave their villages behind? Is their culture at risk of disappearing forever? Will their village become one of those abandoned ruins I'd seen on our trek? Ever since my conversations with Sonam Dorje back in Phu, I'd been wrestling with these dilemmas, and they had become even more troubling to me once I'd met Karma and began helping her, and now Pemba, to get an education. But never had I been faced with them as forcefully as I was then, when I was confronted with the very real possibility their culture might be destined one day to be nothing more than a diorama in a museum.

However, what happened next brought a new thought to me. Near the end of our tour, we came upon a Tibetan Buddhist shrine hall, elaborately fashioned after that of a traditional gompa. Without any instruction or prompting, Karma and Pemba approached the shrine and with eyes closed placed their hands in prayer position, touched their hands to their temples, to their lips, and then to their hearts, while offering the Tibetan blessing, *Namo Buddaya, Namo Dharmaya,* and *Namo Sanghaya* (homage to the Buddha, the teachings, and the community). They remained there for a moment, in profound thought, with eyes still closed, before they stepped backwards from the shrine. I saw in that action that their culture and its traditions are something that will always reside within them. Then I remembered Sonam had said to me, the first time we met, that for him the most important thing was that his girls never forget where they're from, never forget their Dharma, their way of being. I realized as I watched Karma and Pemba that, thanks to the way they were raised, they will not forget. It has become part of the very essence of who they are.

"There are some things that should not change," I said to Sonam. I don't know if he understood me, but his eyes seemed in agreement.

TWENTY-FOUR

I felt like I needed to climb a mountain. Chantal and I were scarcely home a week, and the burden of our last journey to Nepal – the reality of all the devastation and suffering – was weighing heavily on me. It was late October and beginning to feel like fall in Vancouver. Leaves had turned orange and red, the days were growing shorter and the air was crisp. Normally, fall weather is unpredictable on the west coast, often with lengthy periods of rain. Yet the sun was predicted to hold for the coming days, giving us the perfect weather window to climb something.

A couple of friends didn't need much convincing, so the three of us made a plan to climb Sky Pilot Mountain the following day. It was a beautiful mountain, not far from us, and one I was intimately familiar with. It provided a little bit of everything: an approach through old-growth forest, an ascent of a glacier and an aesthetically enjoyable scramble up decent rock to the summit. And because it was one of the highest peaks in the area, it offered stunning views over our coast and the surrounding ranges. I was exhilarated by the thought of being on it again.

Yet the day before we were to embark, something felt off. A strange sensation of uneasiness began to grow within me. I knew it wasn't an overly technically difficult mountain, and conditions were in our favour. Yet the feeling persisted. It lasted the entire day, so much so that I bought a new rope for the trip and put out my first aid kit with weighed intention. Later that evening, Chantal asked me what was wrong. I was usually eager the night before a climb. This time I had a foreboding feeling about the whole thing, but I couldn't explain it. I figured there was no sense in worrying about it, and the best thing was to get some sleep before our early start.

Very early the next morning I woke up to get ready, and the feeling was still there. Nonetheless, my two friends Adam and Garrett and I left for the mountain. It felt good to get out; the cool breeze on the face, the fresh scent of the alpine, the thick clean air in the lungs. We kept a brisk pace through the forest as traces of morning sun began to push light through the trees. The feeling of apprehension subsided a little, perhaps because the splendour of nature was so overwhelmingly healing.

Before long we reached the edge of the glacier, where we stopped for a quick drink and put on our crampons. The glacier, although not very steep, was completely bare of snow, leaving its icy blue surface as smooth as an ice cube and as hard as concrete. But I wasn't worried because our crampons were rigid and their steel teeth would bite. I stepped on the glacier. The feeling within me came back in full force, spreading immediately throughout my entire body. Something was wrong. I scanned the ridgeline. Apart from some rock hazards, I couldn't detect any other possible risks. What was going on? I had warning signals go off only once before, years ago, when a friend and I were rappelling down a mountain. As I had reached the ledge and begun to unhook my rappel device, a voice inside my ear whispered for me to look up. Without much thought I obeyed, only to see the rope had dislodged a golf-ball-sized rock that was whizzing directly toward my face. Reflexes took over and I jerked my head to the left. I felt a whoosh of air brushing my right ear as the rock went by, a sensation I will never forget.

Yet this time was somehow different. I didn't hear any whispers in my ear. I only felt a nagging uneasiness, a tingling in my heart that left me with a strong sense of foreboding. But that was enough for me. *I'm listening to this feeling. I'm out.* I looked to Adam and Garrett. "You guys go ahead. I'm going to stay here."

The two of them stopped, taken off guard, and looking a little uneasy about my decision.

"Mike, what is it?"

"I'm just not feeling it today. I'm happy to stay here."

Adam and Garrett searched around as though there was some un-detected danger they couldn't see. For the next ten minutes we deliber-ated about what to do. But I was unable to articulate what I was feeling. It didn't help that I didn't know what it was I was feeling. So we agreed the logical thing to do was to resume climbing the glacier and stop every ten minutes to reassess. That sounded reasonable. We proceeded to climb. We stepped aggressively into the ice with our crampons, moving up the mountain one step at a time. Everything seemed to be okay, and no dan-ger appeared present. We neared the top of the glacier, where it steep-ened the most, folding into the rocky ridge above. Another party of two approached from below and began angling along the steep ice toward us. Adam made his way onto the rock, and then Garrett, and in a few steps, I would be there too.

And then it happened. I heard a sound and looked over my left shoul-der to see what it was, but I already knew. One of the climbers behind us had lost his footing and was rocketing uncontrollably down the glacier. I couldn't believe what I was seeing. He fell helplessly for two hundred me-tres before coming to a stop. I looked to Adam and Garrett. They looked as though they had seen a ghost.

"Are you all right?" I yelled down the mountain.

A faint voice came back, still in shock. "Yes. I think…I think I'm all right."

I felt my heart racing as I breathed a huge sigh of relief. I resumed mak-ing my way toward the rock, kicking my front points into the ice. It must have been less than 20 seconds later that I heard the noise of crampons slipping on ice, and that dreaded sound again. Oh my god. I looked over my left shoulder. The second climber had lost his footing and was now rocketing down the mountainside. *I am not seeing this. This is not happen-ing again.* My eyes stayed fixed on him, unable to look away. Everything fell silent. My world became entirely still, and all I could focus on was the falling man. I could see nothing else. I could hear nothing else. His cram-pons caught in the ice, flipping him forward. He must have been travel-ling over 40 kilometres an hour when he flew face first into a boulder. Like a lifeless marionette, he tumbled round and round for another hundred metres or so before coming to rest near his friend. My eyes stayed fixated on him until, as though from a great distance, a voice above me began to make itself heard.

"Mike! Mike!" Garrett was shouting for me to make my way up. Those remaining steps took every ounce of mental strength I had, and then at last the three of us were safe on the rock. Fortunately, we had mobile coverage and called 911. The second climber was unconscious, and from below I could hear him bellowing moans that were sickening in their intensity. The first climber lay still on the ice, unable to move.

Garrett had been on search and rescue for several years, so I gave him my first aid kit and we used our rope to belay him down to where the second climber lay. There was blood everywhere and the climber's face was shattered. Garrett placed his backpack under the climber's body to lift him partially from the ice, and held his head in an open airway position to prevent him from choking on his own blood.

Within 30 minutes, helicopters arrived and the fallen climbers were extricated. We learned that the two had just met in a meet-up group that morning and had little experience in the mountains. The first climber ended up walking away with a broken arm and a deep gash on his hip. The second climber, unfortunately, never regained consciousness and remains on life support.

Minutes turned into hours and we made our way down the mountain. Hours turned into days. Days turned into weeks. I was still trying to process what had happened. Search and rescue organized a debriefing session for us, and even followed up with calls to see how each of us was doing. Everything seemed to be fine. That is, until one day I was driving home and felt as though I was about to erupt into tears and my chest was going to burst. Then, in less than a second, the sensations vanished as though they'd never been there. The same thing happened two or three more times over the course of several days, so I decided the best thing for me would be to get back into the saddle, and fast.

The following weekend Chantal and I went out to climb an easier mountain. We found ourselves on a steep snow slope. Partway up, I froze. Somehow my body seized up and I couldn't move my legs. All I could see when I closed my eyes was the image of the limp flailing body plummeting down the mountain. I felt my knuckles whitening around the head of my ice axe.

"Mike, what's wrong?"

The truth is I didn't know what was wrong, only that it wasn't normal. I didn't have the tools to deal with this, and knew I needed help. Chantal recommended a therapist to me, someone who had helped her with some of her migraine and anxiety-related challenges. The therapist was trained in the art of Hakomi therapy, a psychotherapy practice designed to access one's deepest emotional state through mindfulness. What did I have to lose?

I entered the small, simple, Zen space and sat down on the sofa. A small table was on my right, and a box of tissues was to my left. Across from me, the therapist sat in her chair. And then we began. The process lasted over an hour, and by the end she had unlocked a store of emotions that had been hidden deep within me. The emotions had become so tightly shackled to my subconscious that, when they were released, tears erupted from my eyes and I could feel the energy of thousands of micro-vibrations reverberating throughout my body. My tongue and jaw shook so violently I felt as though I was being electrocuted. And then, to my astonishment, it was over. I was light again. The therapist explained that, when I witnessed the fall, I myself was still in a precarious position, so in order to get myself to safety I had to suppress and internalize my emotions, locking them up so they wouldn't affect my actions. Now it was safe to release them, which she had helped me to do. But that was only part of the healing. I also had to learn to put some distance between myself and what I'd witnessed. When I watched the falls occur, I felt a sense of profound horror, and this heightened emotional state had caused my subconscious to fuse what I saw to my very sense of self. The therapist took me through an exercise of deep mindfulness to enable me to separate what I saw from who I am.

Before I left, I asked the therapist about the premonition I felt before the accident, but she didn't have an explanation for it. In talking about it to friends later, however, I heard various theories. One person suggested that because time is not linear I might have tapped into a "future" event in the "present." Another man, someone who is a good friend and a member of the Tahltan First Nation, said he believed it was my ancestors speaking to me. "What are you going to do to honour it?" he asked. This was an intriguing question.

I do know one thing for sure – whatever such feelings are, wherever they come from, whether it's the past or the future or some timeless dimension, under no circumstances will I ever second-guess them again. If something doesn't feel right to me, I will listen to that warning – "honour" it, as my First Nation friend says.

Perhaps some things are not meant to be understood with the rational mind and exist only at a deeper level of consciousness. Our eyes and ears can only see and hear a tiny spectrum of the known colours and frequencies. So why shouldn't this be true for our minds as well?

I feel that way also about the deep connection Chantal and I have with Karma and Pemba and their family, and about all the uncanny links and correspondences I experienced when I first went to Nepal. I don't understand them, but I feel them, and I know they were meant to be. By honouring them, I have greatly enriched my life.

TWENTY-FIVE

Sometimes the right decision is the hardest one to make. The more Chantal and I visited Nepal, the more we struggled with what the best course of action would be for Karma and Pemba's future education. We were caught in the clash of two worlds. We lived in one of the wealthiest countries in the world, and they lived in one of the poorest. Yet where our culture was rich in some things, theirs was rich in others, including the kindness and generosity, the courage and resilience, we'd seen among the people we'd met in the mountains. However, in Nepal there were so many obstacles stacked against them – the earthquake and the devastation of Kathmandu that would take years, perhaps decades, to recover from; the political turmoil; the cultural discrimination they would have to endure in Nepal's caste-driven society – that my first reaction was to bring them to Canada as soon as possible. To bring them out of the pollution and the chaos of Kathmandu. To give them the same opportunities as children in our country have. Yet every time Chantal and I returned to Nepal, the Canadian scales fell from our eyes and we saw past the poverty to the inner richness and beauty of the Nepali people.

It was frustrating to try to reconcile the fundamental imbalances in our world, never knowing what was the right thing to do. On the one hand, Karma's computer science class consisted of her studying a textbook that looked like it was from the 1980s, with explanations of the difference between "inputs" and "outputs" and pictures of old desktop computers and dot matrix printers. Meanwhile, kids her age in Canada were learning how to use Google Docs and various web design builders – when they weren't shooting videos on their cellphones. Was it right to let Karma and Pemba fall so far behind? On the other hand, as I was helping Pemba with her Tibetan homework (which mainly consisted of my watching her toil away with extraordinary diligence and skill), she penned the most striking Tibetan calligraphy. Her hand moved gracefully over the page, her focus unwavering. I had no idea what she was writing, but it was an artistic masterpiece if ever I've seen one.

Over the years, I began noticing more and more contrasts between the values nurtured by the environments in Canadian schools (and families) and those at SMD: competition versus collaboration, individuality versus community, pride versus humility, judgment versus empathy, learning how to get more versus learning how to let go. Our culture provides an abundance of opportunities for material goods and experiences, including access to higher education, as well as all the basic necessities: health care, a safe environment, transportation, clean air and water (in 2018 Kathmandu was ranked last among 180 countries for air quality, with air pollution as a leading threat to public health).[20] But what would be the trade-off? At SMD they learned the Dharma, cultivating qualities of mindfulness, spiritual awareness and emotional intelligence at a depth I had never seen before.

Yet I couldn't help wonder whether this was a privileged First World question even to be asking. Anyone surviving in the lower quadrants of Maslow's hierarchy of needs wouldn't have the luxury of debating such choices. We have so much over here – too much. Should we not be sharing it with those who have less? When we discussed this with others, parents and non-parents alike, in Nepal and Canada, as well as elsewhere in the world, they offered us a full spectrum of differing opinions. Some said without hesitation that life in Canada would be better for Karma and Pemba. Most of those we spoke with from India or Nepal thought the answer was a no-brainer – of course, we should bring the children to a First World country. The wealthier Nepalis themselves didn't hesitate to send their children to other more privileged countries for their education. Occasionally, someone would say it would probably be best for them to stay in Nepal, so they could help their own country. Yet this rationale wasn't convincing to me, because so many of the Nepalis I had come to know in North America continued to help their countries from abroad, including Tashi, the young SMD graduate who had brought us to meet Thrangu Rinpoche, and her sister Nangsal. Along with other SMD students who were studying in Canada, they had banded together to organize and lead a fundraiser after the earthquake, specifically for the benefit of the remote mountain villages near the epicentre of the quake. This was important, because the major NGO earthquake relief efforts had all concentrated on the needs of the large urban areas of Nepal, leaving many of the mountain villages to fend for themselves.

Another young Nepali, Dolma, a recent graduate of SMD who was studying in the United States and is from the same village as Karma and Pemba, had obtained a $10,000 grant to establish the first health care clinic in Nar. I asked Dolma which country she identified with the most as her home. Neither, she said. While she was born in Nepal, she said that, culturally, she felt more Tibetan. But because she has never been to Tibet she doesn't identify with that country either. "I suppose I feel mostly as though my country is my village of Nar," she concluded. Because a rare opportunity had enabled her to finish her university education in the US, she had chosen to help her village from overseas. I wondered if Karma and Pemba would feel the same.

Chantal and I continued to wrestle with the options for Karma and Pemba. Immediately after the earthquake, we had tried to get them visitor visas to Canada, not just because we wanted them to have a brief escape from the misery of their country but also so they could get a taste of life in Canada. That way they'd be able to decide if they liked it enough to want to study here some day. But that hadn't worked. Our application had been denied for the flimsiest of reasons. Having since spoken to several immigration lawyers and consultants in Canada, we now knew it was easier to get student visas than visitor visas – but still extremely difficult. The bureaucratic obstacles were enormous. So we were left with the understanding that, even if it was ultimately decided that bringing the girls to Canada was the right thing to do, it might not be possible.

And then one day, in the midst of all these deliberations, I received a message from Dawa Tashi, the girls' monk cousin, who was our primary liaison with the family in Nepal and to whom we had grown close over the years. He had good news to share – he had been granted a great honour within the monastery, having been selected as one of eight monks to go into "retreat" – which represents attaining a higher level of Buddhist education. For Dawa Tashi, it meant he would be meditating in total seclusion, with no access to social media or contact with the outside world, for four years. We received what I believe was his last email:

> Dear Mike and Chantal,
> Tashi delek and Namaste. I like to kindly let you know that from today I am entering my four years meditation. … As we know education is very important to the human life so in Nepal we cannot get enough education, so Karma and Pemba and their parents will very happy if they get high education in Canada because they really want their children's bright future with great education. Therefore I would like to hearty request you to help them. It is really my hearty request to both of you. Your help brings their great future. Your Dharma friend, DT.

Even after receiving this message, Chantal and I remained uncertain. We finally concluded that the best way to make a decision would be for us to bring Karma and Pemba back to their home village and discuss it with their parents and sisters. Gathering together around their stove, we would be able to come up with the best plan for the girls' future. We set down in writing the three possible options, and asked the teacher from whom we had been taking Nepali language lessons in Canada to translate them into Nepali, so we could present the options to them when we returned to Nepal. The first option was that we would support the girls for the entirety of their education in Nepal, however far they wanted to go. For the second option, we would provide for Karma and Pemba to continue at SMD until they graduated Grade 10 (which was as far as SMD went), and then they could come to Canada on study permits to finish Grades 11 and 12, with the possibility of going on to university in either Canada or internationally. For the third option, we would apply for Canadian study permits for Karma and Pemba as early as the following year, 2018. If they chose the third option, and the girls came to Canada, we would bring them to live with us in our home, and we would care for them as our own. We would continue to provide them with Nepali language lessons, as well as regular Tibetan and Dharma lessons at Thrangu Rinpoche's monastery in Vancouver. We would also celebrate all the national Nepali festivals with them, and bring them back to their village every two years. But we also explained in the letter there were no guarantees we would be able to get the necessary student visas to come to Canada, as they are very difficult to obtain.

And then, after all our agonizing, having come to this conclusion, I finally realized I could let go of the outcome. What was best for the girls would be in the hands of their family. Whatever the family decided, Chantal and I would accept with open hearts.

Nar Phu Valley route map, oil on canvas, Jason Kamin, 2020

Burning ghats (cremations) at the holy temples of Pashupatinath
AREK SACZUK, 2012

TOP Sunrise in Boudhanath, Kathmandu
MICHAEL SCHAUCH, 2016

BOTTOM Karma and Pemba with their parents Sonam and Pema, shortly before our first planned departure to Canada – their parents came down from Nar to see them off
MICHAEL SCHAUCH, 2017

195

THIS PAGE TOP The great Boudhanath Stupa
MICHAEL SCHAUCH, 2017

THIS PAGE BOTTOM The Mighty Annapurna Massif
AREK SACZUK, 2012

OPPOSITE Terraced planting fields along the Annapurna trail
AREK SACZUK, 2012

OPPOSITE TOP Trail leading to Nar Village
AREK SACZUK, 2012

OPPOSITE BOTTOM The Gates of Phu, entrance into the sacred beyul valley of Phu
AREK SACZUK, 2012

THIS PAGE TOP Children of Phu Village
CHANTAL SCHAUCH, 2012

THIS PAGE BOTTOM Women of Phu working their fields
CHANTAL SCHAUCH, 2012

Phu villager dressed in traditional Chuba
AREK SACZUK, 2012

OPPOSITE TOP Himalayan giants towering over the ruins of Old Phu
MICHAEL SCHAUCH, 2012

OPPOSITE BOTTOM Mike and Chantal before the gates of the Tashi Lhakhang
Monastery
AREK SACZUK, 2012

THIS PAGE TOP Phu Village
AREK SACZUK, 2012

THIS PAGE BOTTOM Dawa Sherpa and Mike
AREK SACZUK, 2012

OPPOSITE PAGE TOP The team's camp in Phu, set in a farmer's field
AREK SACZUK, 2012

OPPOSITE PAGE BOTTOM One of the dinner gatherings we were invited to in Phu
AREK SACZUK, 2012

THIS PAGE TOP The "Phu crew": (left to right) Arek, Jason, Michael, Sonam Dorje, and Mike
CHANTAL SCHAUCH, 2012

THIS PAGE BOTTOM Villagers of Phu at work
AREK SACZUK, 2012

OPPOSITE TOP Karma teaching English numbers to her class
CHANTAL SCHAUCH, 2012

OPPOSITE BOTTOM Karma and her friends after school, shortly after they found our camp
CHANTAL SCHAUCH, 2012

THIS PAGE TOP The Nar Entrance Mani wall – the most magnificent Mani wall we saw during our trek
AREK SACZUK, 2012

THIS PAGE BOTTOM Michael entertaining the school kids of Nar
AREK SACZUK, 2012

OPPOSITE TOP Nar village centre Mani wall
MICHAEL SCHAUCH, 2017

OPPOSITE BOTTOM Mike, still feeling conflicted about leaving his mountain, seeing Nar village for the first time. The 6000-metre Pisang Peak towers behind him.
CHANTAL SCHAUCH, 2012

ABOVE Chantal and Karma embracing after dancing together
AREK SACZUK, 2012

OPPOSITE Pemba in class during our first visit to Nar's school in 2012
AREK SACZUK, 2012

TOP SMD School students with the Venerable Khenchen Thrangu Rinpoche (centre), School Director Shirley Blair (far left), and School Principal Acharya Wangchuk Tenzin (far right)
K. JANGCHUP SMD SCHOOL

BOTTOM SMD Children with Mike and Chantal
SMD STUDENT, 2015

TOP Mike, Pemba, Karma and Chantal at SMD School
PRINCIPAL ACHARYA WANGCHUK TENZIN, 2017

BOTTOM SMD School's central building and playground
CHANTAL SCHAUCH, 2014

OPPOSITE TOP Mike helping Pemba with her homework during a family vacation to Pokhara
CHANTAL SCHAUCH, 2015

OPPOSITE BOTTOM Nar valley and Nar village – several new tea houses (buildings with blue roofs) had appeared since our last visit in 2012
MICHAEL SCHAUCH, 2017

ABOVE A local carrying water pipe up to Nar
MICHAEL SCHAUCH, 2017

TOP Karma and Pemba on horseback, riding back to their village
MICHAEL SCHAUCH, 2017

BOTTOM Nar village
MICHAEL SCHAUCH, 2017

TOP Atop Sonam and Pema's home, where we perched our tent
MICHAEL SCHAUCH, 2017

BOTTOM With Sonam and Pema and family inside their home
NIMA TAMANG

ABOVE Local weaver in Nar village, weaving yak and sheep wool
MICHAEL SCHAUCH, 2017

OPPOSITE TOP One of Nar's monasteries
MICHAEL SCHAUCH, 2017

OPPOSITE BOTTOM Receiving a blessing from the village Lama the morning of
our departure in 2017
NIMA TAMANG, 2017

ABOVE Sonam and Mike the morning of Mike and Chantal's departure from Nar village in 2017
CHANTAL SCHAUCH, 2017

OPPOSITE Karma and Pemba's family waving us a final farewell the morning of our departure from Nar village in 2017
MICHAEL SCHAUCH, 2017

OPPOSITE TOP Karma and Pemba's arrival in Canada, and the first time they set foot on a beach
MICHAEL SCHAUCH, 2018

OPPOSITE BOTTOM Karma and Pemba's first hike in Canada, near our home in Squamish, BC
MICHAEL SCHAUCH, 2018

ABOVE Karma and Pemba taking a break during one of our many hikes near our home in Squamish, BC
MICHAEL SCHAUCH, 2018

ABOVE Mike descending one of his Squamish favourites, Mt. Tantalus
KLEMEN MALI, 2016

OPPOSITE Junu, Pemba and Karma dressed in their celebratory Chubas
at Thrangu Rinpoche's Monastery in Richmond, BC, during Tibetan Losar
(Tibetan New Year's celebration)
MICHAEL SCHAUCH, 2018

TOP Mike and Chantal making their way to the summit of Mt. Garibaldi, the highest peak in the Squamish valley
JAMES FRYSTAK, 2019

BOTTOM Mike and Chantal pausing to watch the sunrise during their ascent of Mt. Garibaldi
JAMES FRYSTAK, 2019

TWENTY-SIX

The Himalayan horses strode forward, sure-footed, eyes never straying from the narrow trail ahead. They were no bigger than mules – much smaller than the horses I was used to in Canada – yet strong like the mountain dwellers we had come to know. Their hair was coarse and thick, their manes long and shaggy. Sonam had strung colourfully woven wool blankets over their backs, tying them snug so they wouldn't shift around on the myriad steep inclines and declines that lay before us. Intricately woven wool bridles and reins were meticulously laced and knotted. Karma and Pemba rode the horses, while the rest of us walked. Although it had been years since the girls had ridden their horses, they hadn't forgotten how. It was as much a part of their muscle memory as riding a bicycle is for children in Canada. Once mastered, never forgotten.

The mountain trail following the winding Phu River was as narrow as I remembered it, often wide enough for only a single horse. It snaked its way high above the valley floor, with sheer cliffs on either side. I thought about the horse carcass we had seen the last time we were here five years ago. The horse had slipped off the trail, falling to the rocks below. I looked to the girls, riding along the same narrow cliffs, and tried to put that thought out of my mind. Back home no parent I knew would have allowed their child to take such a risk. Yet here it was a necessity.

Although it had been five years since Chantal and I last travelled this trail to Nar, the valley felt oddly familiar. This time was very different because we were travelling it with Sonam, Karma and Pemba.

What was also different – very different – was the road we'd taken to get this far. It was astonishing how much had changed on the Annapurna Circuit over the intervening five years. The quaint farming community of Bhulbhule, where we had previously commenced our trek after the long bus ride, was completely unrecognizable. I wouldn't even have known we were in it had our driver not mentioned its name. The site where I had stood under the string of prayer flags, contemplating the journey that lay before us, was now the site of a major Chinese hydroelectric dam. The newly built hydro plant presented quite a contrast to the tin-roofed farmhouses that still remained. Barbed-wire walls quarantined the site, which was watched over by white-gloved Chinese guards in uniform standing at its gates. The whole town had turned into a construction site. Cement factories had torn up the grounds. Dump trucks and heavy machinery dotted the landscape.

Seeing all those changes, I couldn't help wondering who stood to benefit from them. I wondered what had happened to the livelihood and the homes of the villagers who had lived here for generations. I remembered the young girls who had flocked around Chantal the last time we were here, and the little one who was also named Shanti, and wondered where they were now. Was this progress? Perhaps. But at what cost?

The trekking route we had travelled out of Bhulbhule with Arek, Jason and Michael back in 2012 had now been widened into a road. When we passed through here before, it was just being built, and we had seen the military blasting the road out of the rock. It was dangerous work, high above the valley floor, and we'd been told that eight military personnel had died during the construction of this section of the road. But the road – if you could call it that – was a rudimentary and precarious affair consisting mostly of rounded boulders and gravel. Pemba called it the "dancing road." It passed through mountain streams, along steep washouts, over large rocks and deep potholes. Perhaps the scariest section was that above the village of Tal. "We are now entering most dangerous road in all of Nepal," the driver had said to me as we climbed higher up the cliff side. I noticed our guide, Nima, fingering his prayer beads while reciting "om mani padme hum," his eyes tightly closed. Less than six months after we'd passed through that section of road, a jeep ferrying trekkers lost control and tumbled down into the gorge in that same spot, killing one of the trekkers and injuring the other nine.

Rough as it was, the road meant that what had once taken us four days to trek, we had been able to drive in two eight-hour days in our two Toyota Land Cruisers. In addition to Karma and Pemba and our drivers, we had come up from Kathmandu with one porter and a guide. It was still required to have a guide to go into the Nar Phu valley, and we had needed a porter because we were bringing up supplies for the family, plus extra provisions for the girls and ourselves in case we were pinned down by another natural disaster.

The road had become very popular with the locals, who stuffed themselves into jeep "taxis" – often as many as nine or ten people to a vehicle – to ferry themselves and provisions between villages. Because the primitive road was so hard on these taxis, it wasn't uncommon for them to break down, blocking the entire road for hours at a time until they could be fixed. On the second day, one of our own Land Cruisers had broken down. Its wheel axle had completely severed in two. Fortunately, by the time it happened, we were only a couple of kilometres from Koto, our final destination along the Annapurna Circuit before branching off, on foot, up the Nar Phu valley. Chantal and the girls and I crammed ourselves and the provisions into the other Land Cruiser, and the porter and the guide walked the remaining distance to Koto.

The following day we began the trek, knowing we would soon be joining Sonam. He hadn't wanted to come into Koto with the horses, because they spooked when there were too many people around, so the plan was to meet up on the trail after we entered the Lost Valley, north of Koto.

The girls were ecstatic to be going home. They hadn't seen either their mother or their village in over two years. Pemba was so excited she kept breaking into song, composing ballads of her own in her native tongue of Narpa, which then flowed into traditional Nepali songs and Hindi pop songs. She was only 8 years old and could speak four languages. For the entire trip up the Annapurna Circuit, Karma and Pemba had talked nonstop about their home and their village. They told us about all the changes that had occurred there, including the fact that the village now had a mobile phone tower, and their father had installed a toilet in their home. They even had a satellite dish and a TV with one channel. They told us about their planting season, and how they would harvest potatoes and barley. They described their animals – one yak and 12 *pri* (female yaks), and 20-plus goats and sheep – and how they sheared the wool from the sheep and used the goat and sheep dung to fertilize the fields. They also told us about how excited they were to see their sister Nyima and meet her newborn baby, little Dorje. We had met Nyima years ago when she came to the zoo with us. At the time she had been a nun at Thrangu Rinpoche's abbey outside Kathmandu, but we had sensed she was not happy there. Since then she had left the abbey to return to her village and start a family.

Pemba told us about the last time she visited her village, and how they had hiked directly from Koto to Nar for 12 hours, straight through the night. When I asked whether they had headlights or flashlights to illuminate the path, she replied, "We had the moon!" She was 6 years old at the time.

As Karma and Pemba walked side by side along the narrow gorge, chattering to themselves in anticipation, they kept an eye out for their father. Each time a figure approached in the distance, they would subside into silence, waiting in breathless suspense to see if it was Sonam. And then, at last, the bright-spirited man appeared with the girls' horses in tow. The girls seemed almost as excited to see their horses as they were their father – a reminder of the mountain village life they had lived long enough ago that it must have seemed an eternity in their young eyes. Karma's horse was golden brown, and Pemba's was ash grey. Throughout our journey up the Annapurna Circuit, Pemba had explained in great detail how to safely ride a horse along the narrow trails – describing how to position your body as you're descending a steep section or climbing the thin switchbacks. And now we were watching her doing it!

It was hard keeping up with the horses, especially with our heavy packs. The thin air left Chantal and me gasping. Sonam stopped often to let us catch our breath. He offered to send horses down for us too, but we declined, explaining we had to acclimatize by walking. Having driven most of the way instead of trekking, as we had done last time, we hadn't yet become accustomed to the altitude. Fortunately for us, Sonam was a patient man.

Unlike us, Pemba and Karma were having no problems with the altitude. This brought to mind something I had learned from Mark Aldenderfer, an anthropologist and explorer for *National Geographic* who had done a NOVA/PBS documentary called *Secrets of the Sky Tombs*, based on his work studying the sky caves of Nepal. Shortly after returning to Canada from our first trip to Nepal, we had told Mark about the cave tomb we had discovered in Kyang. Using our coordinates, Mark later ventured to Kyang with his team and found the cave. He was able to date the remains back to the years 358 – 199 BCE, which made them over 2,200 years old. Through DNA studies of the bones, Mark had uncovered evidence supporting the theory that the early Himalayan inhabitants possessed a unique evolutionary mutation – a DNA strand that enabled them to carry more red blood cells and hence adapt better at high altitudes. It was a mutation that persisted in the present-day Himalayan mountain dwellers, and helped to explain how they were able to thrive at altitudes that would have weakened those without it.

Before long we neared the site at Dharamshala where we had seen the old woman sleeping, the one who had so curiously examined Chantal's hands and hair. A small restaurant now occupied the spot. And whereas the old woman had been the only person we encountered on the trail the last time, the trail was now teeming with locals and trekkers alike. It appeared that many more Narpas were travelling up and down the valley to Koto to trade and collect supplies.

Mick had been right with his prediction that night in Vancouver. As soon as the valley opened to outsiders, change was inevitable. More mobile towers were being erected, continually expanding the spread of the internet to the farthest reaches of the planet, and televisions and satellite disks were making their way into the villages – as they had in Nar, as Pemba and Karma had just told me.

The roads were also being pushed ever higher into the mountains. On the trail we saw young boys who looked no older than 15 or 16 hammering at the rocks with steel pikes, while others lugged rocks in baskets strapped around their foreheads for several kilometres. It looked like they were extending the road up from the Annapurna Circuit deep into the Nar Phu valley.

After nine hours of hiking, we reached the plateau settlement of Meta. This settlement had also changed. What had once seemed a nearly deserted village, which was mainly a winter residence for the semi-nomadic people of the Lost Valley, was now almost bustling. There were now six tea houses, not one, and there were places for trekkers to stay. Tea houses catering to trekkers seemed to be proliferating everywhere in the mountains. We heard there was even a tea house en route to Phu, and three more in Phu itself. I thought about young Sonam Dorje of Phu, and what he must think about these new developments. They certainly represented a change in the culture, but perhaps he would be happy for his village. Perhaps the increase in tourism would give it a better chance of surviving, and bring amenities that would make the villagers' lives easier. I was sorry not to be able to go to Phu to see him, but we didn't have enough time. I didn't even know if he was still there, since without any means of staying in contact, I'd lost touch with him. I had often wondered how he was doing.

Chantal and I stayed at one of the new tea houses in Meta to give our bodies a chance to acclimatize, while Karma and Pemba rode on with Sonam to another little settlement called Chaap to see their mother, who had brought all the goats and sheep down for the winter to graze. I recalled passing through Chaap on our previous journey. It looked like nothing more than the ruins of a settlement, with only a handful of open stone shelters. Somewhere amid those shelters, their mother Pema would live for much of the season, sleeping on a wool mat on the bare earth.

During our time in Meta, we told our guide, Nima, the story of Karma, and why we were coming back to Nar. Nima was a kind-faced man with a hearty laugh who'd been like a grandpa to the kids on the way up. In his early 60s, he was still tough as nails, which I'd come to see as typical of the mountain people of his age. He came from the Solu Khumbu region near Everest, and hence was culturally similar to Karma and her family.

We told Nima we had written a letter to Karma and Pemba's family, laying out the options for their future, and we asked him if he would be able to read and explain it to them in Nepali, since they probably couldn't read much. He was incredibly touched by what we were doing for Karma and Pemba, and he took the task very much to heart, understanding the gravity of the decision that had to be made. For days Nima practised reciting the letter. He took the weight of the girls' future on his shoulders – so much so that he even appeared stressed about making sure he could read the letter with absolute clarity and accuracy. Yet it was a task he felt honoured to fulfill.

The following morning we trekked toward Chaap, where we reunited with Karma and Pemba and were able to spend time with Pema, whom we had not seen since we met her in her home over five years before. Her skin was weathered and copper-coloured as I remembered, although she didn't look a day older. As for Karma and Pemba, they had metamorphosed back into mountain girls overnight. They had slept on the dirt floor of the stone shelter and smelled of fire and earth. Their clothes were dusty and their hands black with soot and soil. No doubt they had been put to work tending to the flocks of goats and sheep as soon as they arrived.

After joining us for a cup of coffee, Pema returned to the goats and sheep and bid us all farewell. Karma and Pemba would come with Chantal and me to Nar, and Pema would return home to be with us as soon as she could. She would gather her animals and bring them back up to Nar with her in the coming days because a snow leopard had reappeared and was threatening the herds.

Sonam awaited us with the girls' horses on the other side of the Phu River, and we began the steep hike up to Nar. As we plodded forward along the switchbacked mountain trail, ever gaining in elevation, the air became thinner and the land drier. "Man, they live far away," I said under my breath. From the look on Chantal's face, I knew she was thinking the same thing.

Sonam was a thoughtful man. He had arranged for a cousin of Karma and Pemba's to meet us halfway up the trek, bringing food and coffee down from Nar, which we all shared.

Before long, the 7000-metre snow-capped peaks that had lured me years ago made themselves known once again, towering over us. I gazed at them in awe, as always, but this time without any feelings of regret. My mind wandered back to the pyramid mountain, forever etched in my heart. Upon returning from our first excursion into the Nar Phu valley, I discovered the mountain's name – Chako. A Japanese party had climbed it in 2008. Another ascent had been attempted in October 2011 by a Bulgarian team only months before our arrival. But when one of the Bulgarians fell off the mountain and died, the party retreated.

At the top of the climb, we passed through the Nar gate, and over the next rise Nar's grand mani wall awaited us. Stretched out across the Himalayan plateau like a castle wall, gigantic mountains on either side, it was as impressive a sight as I had remembered. Yet this time, as we walked alongside it with Sonam and his cousin, trailing the girls on horseback, it no longer felt as though we were strangers entering a strange land. We had returned to Nar as family.

TWENTY-SEVEN

I stood on the roof of Sonam's house, surveying the Nar valley. Apart from the whisper of the Himalayan winds, nothing broke the early morning stillness of the village. Strings of prayer flags fluttered atop the houses nearby. The mighty snow-capped peaks loomed above. A small pot of burning juniper branches breathed the fresh scent of incense into the air. Each morning Sonam put new juniper into it, offering a blessing for the day.

This was our fourth day of living with Karma and her family. The last time we were in Nar we had observed it as outsiders. The 17th-century rock buildings had been foreign to us, as were the villagers and their ways. This time we were observing it from the inside. Over the past few days, Chantal and I had become a part of Sonam's household. My eyes opened to new details. My senses opened to new vibrations. My mind opened to new thoughts.

Rays of light began illuminating the earthy rooftops around me as the warmth of the sun touched my face. Sonam's roof, like all the others in the village, doubled as a terrace, reached by a sturdy beam of wood with hollowed-out footholds. The terraces were places for socializing, for washing, for drying clothes and for relaxing. They were also where most of the communication between different houses occurred. Villagers often held multiple conversations at once, calling to each other from terrace to terrace, the absence of any other kind of noise allowing their voices to carry the distance. This age-old form of communication continued well into 2017, when we were there, but I couldn't help but wonder when cellphones would replace it.

The flat stones that made up the homes of the village were cool to the touch and coarse. Piles of split firewood lined the outside walls. Stacks of dried cow dung, used for cooking fuel, were sheltered beneath lean-to roofs. Near each house was a stable that housed the family's cows and horses. The toilet Sonam had dug was in a small enclosure inside his stable. While Sonam took immense pride in taking care of his home and keeping it clean, the reality of village life was evident. All the animals dwelt among the houses, often roaming freely. The narrow village paths were a mixture of mud, garbage, sewage and animal feces. There were only three taps with running water for the entire village of roughly 700 residents, and each morning Chantal and I would walk through the muck to the nearest tap for our water.

Initially, Chantal and I had been hesitant when Sonam insisted we stay in his home instead of at the tea house. After all, we weren't sure about their day-to-day customs, nor did we know what we'd be eating every day. But most importantly, we had no idea where everyone would be sleeping. We'd been in their home before and knew it wasn't much bigger than that of a typical bedroom in a Canadian house. With Sonam and Pema, Nyima and her husband and son, Karma and Pemba, our guide Nima and our porter, plus Chantal and me, we would total ten plus a baby. Lhakpa, the eldest sister, and Palma, the middle sister, were away when we arrived, but once they returned, there would be 12! But we couldn't refuse as it would have come off as disrespectful. And it offered us a chance to truly immerse ourselves in village life. As the Nepali way had taught us, we let go of the outcome and decided to let things unravel as they might. Fortunately, we were able to pitch our tent on Sonam's roof, which worked out perfectly. Nima and the porter slept in a small room outside the main house, just big enough for the two of them to lie down. Living with our Nepali family, as it turned out, was one of the most unforgettable experiences of my life.

Next to me, smoke began to billow from the cylindrical tin chimney, signifying that breakfast was being prepared inside Sonam's house below. Sonam and his family had deeply cared for us over the past four days.

Each day, they prepared and served breakfast, lunch and dinner, and as we were their guests, they insisted we not lift a finger with the cooking or cleaning. Nyima always took charge of the cooking, usually with the help of her cousin or sisters, who pitched in with their own homemade ingredients, and the meal preparations were treated as social events. Breakfast usually consisted of *tsampa*, a kneaded mixture of barley flour and butter tea. For lunch, we would have a variation of *dhal bhat* – lentils and rice with potatoes, sometimes mixed with chillies and garlic. Dinner would either be momos (potato-filled dumplings) or *thukpa*, a noodle soup mixed with onions and garlic. Sometimes a little dried yak meat would be mixed in. Sonam would slice it into pieces, swiftly and skilfully striking the rock-hard meat with the inverted blade of his gurkha kukri knife, just millimetres from his fingers. Everything was made from scratch with their own ingredients, and, with the exception of the rice, they grew and harvested all their own food. They were the best meals I had eaten in all of Nepal.

Sonam was a leader in his community and well respected in the village. He loved his family very much, and was very proud of his home, people and culture. He also took great care to make sure we were comfortable at all times. Each morning, he would climb the wood beam ladder, and after lighting the juniper branches he would wipe down our tent from the evening dew and dust. He would then clean the tarp he had placed in front of our tent, and bring out his yak hides and blankets so we all had a place to sit in the sun.

Because it was shoulder season, planting had not yet begun, and Sonam's yaks were still in a lower valley for grazing. This meant he had time to spend with us. Each day we hiked up different hills surrounding the village to get new perspectives and greater insights into their valley. He took us to the north, showing us the locals' routes – hidden paths to Mustang and Phu, and another to Tibet. He took us to the east, showing us the decrepit mobile phone tower, which had broken down and was awaiting a new part. He showed us where they took the yaks to graze in the winter. He showed us the village burial grounds, where the local lama would decide either to cremate the dead, or, if he deemed it better for the next life, to offer a sky burial, which involved his chopping the body into pieces and placing them on a large rock slab, where they would await the griffons. He took us to the west, showing us the way to the Kang La Pass, where we spotted several herds of bharal. He also showed us their trade routes, and explained how the Nar yaks yielded higher returns in trade than those of the neighbouring valleys because they were better quality. He showed us all five of the village's monasteries and explained how the monasteries were used by different tribes within Nar.

Nar was made up of three tribes, he said, and it was traditional for people to marry across tribes, never intermarrying within their own. He explained many of the village customs and traditions: marital and family conventions, the rules of inheritance, their planting and irrigation methods, how village decisions were made and the history of the settlement. Our guide, Nima, who happily accompanied us on all the excursions, translated for us. But much to our surprise, Sonam had somehow managed to teach himself some basic English over the past few years in his village.

Pemba and Karma joined us on these excursions too, proudly showing us around and displaying their knowledge of their village practices – in English. Their level of maturity yet again amazed me. Pemba was still just a child, but at the age of 8 she could already handle herself on a horse, fixing the saddle, stirrups and bridle, and help her sisters prepare meals and clean the house without any instruction. She even took care of her 8-month-old nephew, swaddling him in a cloth blanket she wrapped around her back. They were still children. Yet they had learned the village way of life as soon as they could walk.

One day we passed Karma's old school, where we had first met Karma and Pemba. Where we had witnessed Karma, 7 years old at the time, proudly teaching her class. Where Chantal and Karma had danced before the towering mountains. And where the karmic spark among the three of us had ignited. Karma had no desire to go back and visit the old school. If anything she seemed a bit dismayed at the very sight of it, for it had not even scratched the surface of Grade 1. However, her teacher spotted us and, having remembered us from that earlier visit, approached me. He had learned of our relationship with Karma and Pemba and their family.

By now word of our presence had made its way throughout the entire village.

"Why? Why these two? Why this family? Why do you do what you are doing?" he asked, his eyes searching mine intensely, as though he sought the clue to some strange mystery that was locked deep within my mind.

As I would discover, it was a question that was on the minds of a number of the families in the village. Why not their own kids? It was a question I'd never asked myself until they did. Truth be told, it wasn't even a decision. The path we had taken had been laid out for us far before we had even arrived in Nar, which was why I'd been prevented from climbing my mountain. It was about Sonam and Pema. It was about how they had raised their children, the love they gave them. It was about the values embedded within Karma and Pemba, and the strength, kindness and compassion the whole family possessed. It was about who Chantal and I were, our journey together and all the choices and circumstances that had led us to Nar. It was about the infinite incremental movements and motions that had caused all our paths to converge. All any of us did was to have the courage to trust where our hearts were leading us.

* * *

Soft footsteps climbed the wooden ladder leading up to the roof. It was Nima, our guide.

"Mike, today, all family members have come to Nar." He was right. With the exception of Karma and Pemba's older sister Wangyal, who was in *shedra* (advanced Tibetan Buddhist studies) in Lumbini, everyone was now home. Karma and Pemba's sisters Lhakpa and Palma had arrived with provisions, and Pema had left the goats and sheep in the care of a friend and returned from Chaap – carrying the family cat in a bag.

We had told Nima it was important for Chantal and me that the whole family be present when we discussed Karma and Pemba's future, so they could all come to a decision together.

"We give letter today?"

"Yes, Nima. Let's give the letter today."

I had no idea what their family would choose for the girls. All I knew was that Chantal and I were prepared to wholeheartedly support whichever option they chose, knowing it would be the best for the girls. I took a deep breath, filling my lungs with mountain air, and together we descended the ladder.

TWENTY-EIGHT

Nima's voice was calm and deliberate. He spoke slowly in his Nepali tongue, articulating with great delicacy each of the words written in our letter, as though he were reciting a fine piece of scripture. Cross-legged and knees touching, we all huddled around the dung-fuelled stove, listening patiently to his reading. Sonam sat in his usual spot to the immediate right of the stove, listening attentively as Nima made his way through the various options: first that Karma and Pemba would stay in Nepal for their education; second that the girls would finish Grade 10 in Nepal, and then come to Canada for the two final high school years and then university; and third – here he paused for a moment, as if considering the enormity of what was being proposed – that the girls would come to Canada as early as the following year.

Chantal and I had learned enough Nepali to understand a few of the words, and from what we could tell Nima was very clear about our commitment to care for the girls as our own if they came to Canada, and to keep them in touch with their heritage through regular Tibetan, Nepali and Dharma lessons at Thrangu Rinpoche's monastery in Vancouver. He also made it clear that, no matter what they chose, we couldn't guarantee that we could get the necessary student visas to bring the girls to Canada.

Sonam spoke his first few words after Nima finished his reading of the three options, asking Nima to repeat the third option, which Nima did, with as much care and precision as he had the first time. My leg rested against Chantal's. We could feel each other's energy. My heart began to beat faster. Chantal's did too. Nima then read the final sentences of the letter, in which we said they didn't have to decide immediately. They should take whatever time they needed to make up their minds.

Sonam turned to Pema, and together they began conversing in Narpa.

"And now they speak their own language," Nima said, no longer able to understand them.

About 30 seconds went by, when Sonam turned to me and said a few words in Nepali. Sonam and Pema had decided. It seemed as though they had already discussed this long before we had even written the letter.

I looked to Nima, and he looked to me. "They choose option three."

Chantal and I turned our gaze to Sonam and Pema. We must have looked surprised. For some reason, both of us had it in our minds they would choose option two – for Karma and Pemba to come later, when they were older, and their culture more deeply imprinted.

"Are they sure?" I asked. "It doesn't have to be next year. It can be as early as next year, but it can also be two or three years out."

Nima repeated my question to Sonam, to which Sonam replied in a few words. Pema added something to Sonam's words.

Nima turned back to Chantal and me. "No, he agrees that next year is best. He says that if they are older, they will be more set in their ways. Maybe when they're older they will no longer want to come. He says he has taken them as far as he can, and now, they have the opportunity to learn more from you. Sonam feels like they will be able to go much further in their lives because of this." Tears began welling in my eyes. "Also, Pema says that before she could not stay connected with them, and that they felt so far away. But now, with the mobile tower in the village and Facebook she can get updates, and speak with them more regularly."

"What about the sisters, what do they think?" Chantal asked.

Nima asked Karma and Pemba's sisters. Lhakpa, Nyima and Palma each replied in her own time. "They are all in agreement. They think this is the best for Karma and Pemba, and they are very happy and thankful for what you are doing for their sisters."

Chantal looked directly to Karma and Pemba. "Karma, what about you? Would you like this? And you, Pemba?"

Pemba interjected a resounding "*Huncha*!" ("Absolutely!"). Karma, giving us her answer with her eyes and a shy grin before putting it into words – English words – said, "Yes, I am excited to come to Canada."

* * *

The sun was sinking behind the hills to the west as Chantal and I wandered the pathways of Nar. We were overcome by emotion. Over the past five years, we had tried so hard to make sense of it all – to understand what was best for two little girls in this strange and uncertain world, to reconcile the conflicting values of our cultures, to find the right way. But perhaps we weren't meant to understand some things. Perhaps all we needed to do was listen to the unspoken language of the heart. Lama Tashi had said that by practising compassion and kindness "we free ourselves from our own mind, from our own prejudices, and from our own view." Perhaps that was what had made it possible for us to step back and let things unfold as they would. I could never have imagined the events we had lived through since our first expedition to Nepal, and yet something about it all felt incredibly right, as though my life had always been heading toward this very moment.

Chantal and I made our way to the eastern outskirts of the village. White clouds lightly dusted the evening sky. Turning back to the west, we saw a distant peak surrounded by a glowing halo of orange and crimson from the setting sun. Beneath the peak rose the silhouetted spire of one of the village monasteries. In the distance, layers of hills seemed to lap the horizon like waves. For an instant, it felt as though eternity could be witnessed in a single sunset. In that moment, everything made sense.

I held Chantal tightly, and she me, as we watched the glow of the sun fade to darkness.

"Mike, what just happened?"

"I don't know. But I'm thankful it did."

TWENTY-NINE

The sun radiated its warmth, and the blue sky shone deep like the sea. Not a cloud could be seen. The ice from the giant mountains sparkled in the dawning light. It was the morning of our departure. Over the next few days, Chantal and I would be journeying the long way back to Kathmandu, and then flying back to Canada. Karma and Pemba would stay in Nar with their family, as they still had a few more days before school resumed.

Following a hearty breakfast of tsampa and yak milk crackers, we methodically packed up all our stuff. Sonam, ever attentive, helped us to collapse and wash down our tent, and hung various articles out to dry from the morning dew. He then invited us up to his rooftop for one final farewell. Sonam and the village lama, who was Dawa Tashi's father, had arranged a special blessing for our journey home. Pemba followed, carrying the prayer scriptures. We suddenly found ourselves on the roof with about a dozen Nar villagers, as well as most of Sonam and Pema's extended family. Khata after khata, the Tibetan silk ceremonial scarves representing compassion and purity, were presented to Chantal and me. We bowed our heads as the scarves were placed around our necks, followed by heartfelt wishes from each villager who adorned us. Nima received an equal share of khatas, until the three of us each had about ten khatas draped around us. After that ceremony, the lama proceeded with the prayers, touching the Tibetan scriptures first to Chantal's forehead, then to mine, uttering Tibetan mantras in a deep prayer voice that silenced the wind and calmed the mountains. It was all I could do to hold back my tears.

Sonam then gifted me an intricately engraved yak horn, hand-carved by his grandfather, the village lama at that time, who had made it into an ink container into which he dipped his pen to write scriptures. Wanting to reciprocate, I took the Leatherman multi-tool from my belt and gifted it to Sonam. And then the two of us embraced as we had never done before. It wasn't customary in their culture to hug, but he had learned some of our ways, as I had learned some of his. We held each other tightly for nearly a minute.

Sonam, Karma, Pemba and their sister Palma then walked us to the Nar gate. As we made our way to the outermost border of the village, more villagers approached and adorned us with yet more khatas and blessings. One of the Elders had a hand-held prayer wheel on a stick that he shook back and forth, while gently touching his forehead to mine, and then to Chantal's. I had no idea what he was saying as he prayed aloud. I didn't need to. I could feel his meaning.

We reached the Nar gate, and embraced Sonam and the girls one last time. Pemba wouldn't let go of my hand, grasping tightly. Every doubt I had ever had over the past five years about what we were doing evaporated in an instant, replaced with a deep sense of gratitude for everything that had brought us to this moment.

We made our way along the mountain path, further and further from the gates. Unable to take our eyes away from them, we kept looking back to Sonam and the girls as they stood there, arms waving in the air, becoming smaller and smaller the further we walked, until they were hardly recognizable in the distance. Yet still they stood by the gates. Still waving their arms.

And then we rounded one last bend in the hillside, and they were gone. As we passed the many chortens and mani walls, we tied our khatas around the stones. Leaving Nar, the same emotions I had felt on our first visit came flooding back. Every step I took away from Nar was another step away from Karma – and Pemba. Yet this time I knew that, one way or another, we would be together again soon and closer than ever. It was hard leaving them, but I was at peace.

I tied my last silk khata around a rock and gazed up to the mountains looking down on me – mountains I had come to know as my friends. Just then, it became clear. It was never to their summits they had called me. They were calling me home.

EPILOGUE

It is August 2019, and Chantal and I pause to watch the rising sun break across the horizon, creating an explosion of cloud and colour, a vast spectrum of gold, orange, purple and pink. We're making our way up Mount Garibaldi, an iconic peak – iconic since it's the highest peak in the area and dominates the local skyline from nearly every vantage point around the Squamish Valley. Moving in silence, we had climbed the rocky, glaciated slopes in the dark and cool of the pre-dawn alpine. As we gaze at the sunrise, I feel as though I've just awakened from a deep sleep, still unsure if what I'm living is real or a dream. I know Chantal is experiencing the same kind of disorientation – trying to process everything that has happened in our lives over the past 12 months.

* * *

Upon returning to Canada in 2017, after the momentous conversation we had with Sonam and Pema and their family about whether to bring Karma and Pemba to Canada to pursue their education, Chantal and I immediately got to work on the girls' student visas. We knew it would be challenging, but we didn't expect that getting Karma and Pemba into Canada would require nothing short of a small miracle. This was in part because all Canadian visa applications have to go through the High Commission of Canada in Delhi, India, which purportedly receives up to 40,000 Canadian visa applications *per month*. Given this volume, it is unable to give proper consideration to each one, and so the vast majority are declined, as soon happened with Karma and Pemba. The explanation: the girls had no travel history and the high commission saw "insufficient reason" for them to come to Canada. After six months and the assembling of a stack of 45 hefty documents, we were able to get the girls' visas approved, but even then it took the direct intervention of a high-ranking Canadian government official to make it happen.

Just as we celebrated our victory, believing the hard part was over, the Nepali government barred Karma and Pemba from exiting their own country. We had the extraordinarily bad timing of trying to bring the girls to Canada at precisely the moment when the authorities were cracking down on all sorts of illegal activities, such as bribing, drug trafficking, and, in particular, child trafficking. Nepal has had a shockingly long history of child trafficking, with thousands of women and girls trafficked from Nepal to India and the Middle East each year.[21] In some cases, the girls are sold by their own parents.

Nepal's new government had, quite rightly, taken a hard stance against these atrocities, and, unbeknownst to us until the day of our departure, had initiated a crackdown at the airport just a few weeks prior. But there was no attempt during this transition time to distinguish between the legitimate and the criminal. Instead, there was a blanket prohibition on allowing any minors to leave the country unless accompanied by their parents. It was, of course, impossible for Karma and Pemba's parents to leave the country. They'd never be granted visitor visas for Canada – it had taken us many months just to get the visas for Karma and Pemba. Ironically, the girls were now victims of the new government's attempt to protect its children.

Fortunately, we had made many friends in Nepal during our visits over the past several years, and they came to our aid. After several exhausting weeks navigating the intricacies of the Nepali bureaucracies, with the full support of Karma and Pemba's parents – and Karma and Pemba's own extraordinary poise and equanimity as they endured numerous private interviews with government officials – we were able to obtain ministry support in Nepal, and the girls were at last free to travel.

A year and a half after Chantal and I had last left the village of Nar, we accompanied Karma and Pemba on the long flight from Kathmandu to Vancouver. I often wonder what went through their minds when they saw the Pacific Ocean stretching out beneath them as far as the eye could see, losing itself to the blue-skied horizon – such a stark contrast with the landlocked vertical terrain they had grown up in.

During the year that followed, we watched as the girls embraced their new world with wonder and curiosity, from the sights and sounds of the modern glass city of Vancouver to the riches of the natural world of the west coast, with its old-growth forests, its majestic mountains – not nearly as dramatic as those of their native land – and the seemingly endless open ocean beyond. Even the smallest of details, something as simple as a traffic light at an intersection (there were none in Kathmandu), captured their interest.

In addition to soaking in all the new sights and learning to negotiate the vast cultural differences, they also picked up many new skills. They learned to ride bikes. They learned how to swim. They tried their hand at skiing – both downhill and cross-country, as well as the luge. They learned piano and violin. They marvelled at the Vancouver Symphony during a live performance in one of Vancouver's grand theatres, after which Pemba was inspired to begin to perform her own music, and to dance as well. During her holiday recital, dressed in her traditional Tibetan silk chuba, she sang a Nepali song called "Ama," about a child's love for her mother, and brought the audience to tears.

They learned rock climbing, which they were complete naturals at, of course! Karma even passed her belay test. She began to belay Pemba, and, eventually, strapping sandbags to her harness to help equalize our weights, she belayed me too. Together we scaled local Squamish rock faces up to 20 metres high. The rock climbing brought to life a new quiet confidence in Karma, which I could see radiating to all aspects of her life.

The girls learned a new way of thinking too. Instead of the memorization and regurgitation they were more familiar with, they learned how to cultivate their critical faculties through class engagement, questioning and reasoning.

Most days after school Pemba would spout questions at me faster than I could answer. "Mike, I want to debate with you about climate change," she said one evening. Never in my wildest dreams did I think I would be having such a debate with a 10-year-old. What was perhaps even more startling was that when Pemba first arrived in Canada, she probably understood less than a third of the English she was suddenly being immersed in, yet by the end of the school year, she was among the top students in her class, scoring 100 per cent on her physics test and near 100 per cent on her history tests.

Karma, the child who had first captivated us with her passion for learning, voraciously devoured books from our home library and, once she discovered it, the community library as well. And she began writing beautiful short stories of her own. I was touched to see that all the stories reflected a deep understanding of compassion. Many of them also seemed to be about leaving home and then somehow finding the way back or to a new home, a theme that obviously resonated with her. One I recall was about an alien who crash-landed in a remote farming area on Earth. Everyone in the vicinity feared the alien, but a young girl, seeing how alone and afraid he was, befriended him and slowly introduced him into her community. Once the alien discovered the community was in trouble because it was no longer possible for it to grow seeds in the soil, he knew what to do to make plants grow again. Word of his skills spread across the land, and other communities, which were also having trouble growing seeds, were able to benefit from the alien's skills. In time, the communities banded together to fix the alien's ship, so he could return home. I can only imagine how daunting it must have been for Karma and Pemba to come to a new country, a new home and a new school where they knew no one and could barely speak or read the language, but this story gave me an inkling of how Karma was experiencing the challenges.

Quietly observant at first, hanging back from active participation, Karma and Pemba soon began to find their way. Karma found the courage to read her stories in front of her class, something she had been too terrified to do when she first arrived, and also gave a classroom talk about her school in Kathmandu, describing both how it differed and how it resembled her school in Canada.

Pemba was quick to make friends. Just as in Nepal, she was often the centre of attention, with lots of girls vying for her friendship, but she was always careful to make sure everyone felt included, especially during play dates or class field trips. I found it curious, but not surprising when I thought about it, that her two best friends in Canada were both Indigenous First Nation girls, for the Bhotiya (mountain people of Nepal) are also considered Indigenous.

Both girls quickly immersed themselves in the day-to-day life of our household. Coming from a home where the entire family of eight lived mainly in one room and they had no indoor plumbing, it must have been strange to find themselves in a house where there were multiple bedrooms and bathrooms, a living room and a dining area and a dizzying array of digital gadgetry (washer and dryer, dishwasher, oven, induction cooktop, refrigerator, heater, etc.), but they quickly learned how to operate and take good care of everything. Unlike most Western parents, we never really had to discuss chores. Other than having to be taught how to use all the appliances, they needed no help and approached everything with the same sense of responsibility and co-operation they had learned in their village, and at SMD. They saw themselves as part of a family and team, where everybody was expected to do their part. Without having to be told, they cleaned their own room and bathroom and also pitched in with the vegetable garden, laundry and kitchen tasks.

I'm sure they must have felt overwhelmed by it all at times, but there was rarely a day our home wasn't filled with laughter and giggles, music and dancing. In addition to her love for traditional Nepali music, Pemba's favourite music was the South Korean pop band BTS – think gangster rap meets romantic teen pop – and she would often sing and dance her way through the house all day and night straight until her bedtime. As for mastery of English, they caught on so fast I'd hear the girls alternating languages as readily as if they were flipping through songs on an iPad. Between Narpa, their village language, Nepali, Tibetan, English and bits of Korean and Hindi tossed in, I often lost track of which language they were jabbering in as they recounted various events from the day. One of their favourite games was to have me guess which language they were speaking, an endless source of amusement to them.

We introduced them to Halloween and Christmas, holidays they'd heard of but knew almost nothing about – except for Santa Claus, about whom Pemba was skeptical. Why, I wanted to know. "Because for the last three years I've asked Santa for a cup with my name on it. But he never brought me one." But even as they were learning more and more about our ways, I tried to make sure they remained connected to their own culture. We celebrated the traditional Tibetan and Nepali festivals. At Losar (Tibetan New Year), the most important of the holidays, the girls were thrilled to dress up in their chubas as we all headed down to Thrangu Rinpoche's monastery to receive blessings and offer prayers for the year ahead. As Chantal and I had promised their parents, the four of us paid regular visits to the monastery for Dharma and Tibetan lessons. For over an hour, we would sit cross-legged on cushions, some days practising Tibetan mantras, other days exploring new ways to use meditation as a means to alleviate "false perceptions," "afflicted emotions" and suffering.

After one of our visits, Karma remarked, with some dismay, that many of the young people in Canada don't seem to have the same respect and courtesy toward Elders, or even their parents, as they do in Nepal. On another occasion, as we raced around the house, throwing our shoes and jackets on because we were late for an event, Pemba stopped me in my tracks. "Mike, if we behaved like this in our village, everyone would think we are sick."

How grateful I felt to be learning from these two beautiful souls. New words, new stories and songs, new ways of listening, new ways of seeing, new ways of being: being together was helping all of us to grow.

Over time, Chantal and I began integrating Nepali words into our conversations. We practised Tibetan mantras with the girls, and we even became pros at making traditional Nepali dhal bhat, among other Nepali dishes (led by the girls, of course!). But by far the biggest change we made was that we learned to become parents. We previously had some practice with Junu, a young Nepali woman, also a graduate of SMD, who had arrived in Canada the year prior to attend a nearby boarding school on scholarship. We'd gotten to know Junu during our visits to Kathmandu because once she'd passed her Grade 10 exams, she'd stayed on at SMD, where she was one of Karma's teachers. All the kids who graduate from SMD are encouraged to give one or two years of service, and she'd chosen to do her service at SMD, and then at a nearby monastery, after which she would go to Canada for Grades 11 and 12. However, in order to accept the scholarship she'd been offered, she needed Canadian host parents, and we had agreed to act in that capacity, partly because she was such a kind, hard-working girl, and partly because we knew she would be a valuable mentor and friend to Karma and Pemba once they came to Canada.

However, being parents to 10- and 14-year-old girls was very different from being a part-time host parent to an 18-year-old who lived on campus most of the year. It was strange being thrust into this new world of parenting literally overnight. Suddenly, we found ourselves immersed in a way of life we had heard about from friends but looked on only from afar. Our online calendars exploded with entries that saw us juggling school events, play dates, field trips, doctor and dentist appointments, music lessons, performances, parent-teacher meetings and more activities than we could ever have imagined fitting into our schedules.

For the first few months, Chantal and I spent two to three hours every night tutoring the girls, helping them to catch up on everything they would need to understand their classroom lessons. Some days I would work with Karma on her math skills. Other days, Chantal would help her with European history and religions, which were completely foreign to her since her studies had focused on Asian history and the stories of the Buddha. Once Chantal helped build context for Karma, by relating the histories and timelines, she could then begin to make sense of it all. Pemba's first school assignment had been to read a novel in English, which required me to help her dissect each sentence so she could make sense of this foreign language – its vocabulary, its grammar, its idioms and colloquialisms, and the nuances that can only be mastered after long exposure. Though challenging, it was tremendously rewarding for Chantal and me to see how quickly they were learning and mastering the demands of their new world.

Yet, as parents, we couldn't help but think more deeply about the girls' futures. Only too soon we found ourselves facing the most difficult decision of our lives: whether to keep the girls in Canada until they graduated, or have them return to finish their schooling in Nepal after their eye-opening, year-long immersion in the West.

Although the girls were thriving and their minds clearly opening and growing, Chantal and I began to become concerned about what would happen if they didn't return to Nepal to complete the rigorous tenth-grade government exams and receive Nepal's infamous Secondary Education Examination – often referred to as the "Iron Gate" of Nepal's academic system. Without it, we knew their prospects for a successful future in Nepal would be severely limited, since Nepal doesn't readily recognize a Grade 12 diploma from other countries. In bringing them to Canada, we had wanted to give them options, to offer them opportunities to thrive in both Nepal and Canada – or anywhere else they might eventually choose to go. But it had gradually become clear to us that if they didn't finish their tenth grade in Nepal, as Junu had done before coming to Canada, we might be opening one door while shutting another. The last thing we wanted was for them to be caught between two worlds, with their choices limited rather than expanded. Also, Karma's quiet curiosity, we felt, needed time to continue to develop, without the high pressure to perform in the North American school system. If she didn't make it into college or university here, the Canadian government would not let her stay in the country.

Over weeks and months, Chantal and I had countless discussions and many sleepless nights trying to arrive at the best course of action. We also sought counsel from Shirley back at SMD, as well as Junu, since each of them had an intimate understanding of both worlds. Shirley assured us that if the girls went home, she would make sure there was a place for them at SMD. In our conversations with Junu, she mentioned that the two years she spent after graduating from SMD – first teaching the younger kids at SMD and then teaching the nuns at Thrangu Rinpoche's Tara Abbey – had been critical to her development, increasing her self-confidence, clarifying her passion to be of service to others and solidifying her desire to become a medical doctor.

Gradually, we found ourselves coming to the conclusion that, after they completed their year of school immersion in Canada, it would be best for Pemba and Karma to return to Nepal for the years leading up to their Secondary Education Examinations. However, we weren't taking into account only academic considerations. There's something very special about Himalayan children: their deeply rooted Dharma, their mindfulness, their wisdom and compassion for all living beings, their capacity to open their hearts to others and their ability to inspire others to do the same – all virtues embedded in their culture. And virtues we need more of in our modern world.

Because those virtues were so much a part of who they were, the girls had touched many lives in Canada. One day the mother of one of Pemba's friends approached me to offer her thanks. "Pemba is my daughter's first friend who truly sees her for who she is," she said. On another occasion, Pemba's teacher, invoking the advanced level of mindfulness Pemba demonstrated in her class, asked me, "How do we get more kids to become like Pemba?"

I realized the education Pemba needed most at this stage in her life, when she was only 11, was back in Nepal. Though we paid regular visits to the nearby monastery, she was so young, and had left her home so early, that I feared her language and Dharma lessons weren't enough to provide the continuity needed to sustain and deepen her roots in her own culture. I remembered Sonam's words. "They should always remember where they're from, and always remember their Dharma," he had said to me during our very first meeting, as though he somehow knew I would one day be faced with this question. I thought back to our visit to the mountain museum in Pokhara, where I'd seen a diorama that was a virtual replica of their home. It had reminded me of a way of life and a system of values that was at risk of disappearing – especially as technology and our modern way of life continues to spread across the world. "Some things should not change," I had said to Sonam on that day.

Much as I didn't want to admit it, I knew deep down that the right thing now was for Pemba to be back in her homeland. There her family and teachers and the monks at her school would foster the strengths unique to the Tibetan culture of her upbringing, strengths that would serve her the rest of her life.

Although I knew that at 14 Karma was old enough that her culture, language and Dharma were more solidly anchored, I realized that, in addition to the importance of graduating tenth grade in Nepal, and having more time to develop in Nepal without the pressure of getting a post-secondary education, she would benefit greatly from the kind of experience Junu had gathered, building her self-confidence and strengthening her commitment to give back to her own people. After all, giving service completed the circle of Thrangu Rinpoche's teachings.

Shirley was completely supportive, ensuring that SMD would have space for the girls to return and make them feel right back at home. Even though Chantal and I knew we had made the right decision, sharing this with the girls wasn't easy. One evening, after all of us reminiscing over old pictures from when we first met those many years ago, and the girls recalling stories from their village and family, Chantal and I explained our decision to them as transparently as possible. We also explained that, as with Junu, who had become a role model for them, no longer "Ms. Junu" but "sis Junu," the opportunity for them to return for Grades 11 and 12 and beyond would be there, if they so chose. It was one of the most emotional experiences of my life. For a long while we all simply sat together, holding each other without speaking. The girls quietly shed a few tears as Chantal and I embraced them tightly, holding back our own tears. I couldn't believe their strength and resilience, and their display of acceptance. I had lost track of time, since it was close to midnight, well past their bedtime. But because it was summer holidays, we told the girls they could sleep in, and gently tucked them in.

The next morning, the girls bounced back with a new-found energy, excited to be reuniting with their family and friends at SMD again, and accepting this change with equanimity. "Our experience here will be part of us no matter where we are," was how Pemba put it.

I was reminded again about the difference between our cultures. Here in the West we tend to attach ourselves to our expectations about the future. And when those expectations are not met, we suffer. Since I'd known them, the girls had time and again shown themselves capable of adapting and changing with the flow of events. This latest change in direction was no exception. Having adjusted almost immediately to the idea that they would be returning to school in Nepal, they spent the day brainstorming ideas about improvements they could make at SMD. For starters, they shared with Chantal that they felt the school should have a new music and dance program.

Their family also met the news with equanimity, a very Buddhist response. Since we could only communicate with Sonam and Pema through a translator, we thought it best to share the news first with Wangyal, the sister who is a nun, studying advanced Buddhist philosophy, since she is reasonably fluent in English. Then she could relay it to them. She understood right away. When I asked her if she had any questions, or needed us to clarify anything, her reply was a simple "No. Because you are thinking ahead, of Karma and Pemba's futures. And most people don't do that." We later learned from Wangyal that Sonam and Pema were in agreement, which we were very glad to hear.

* * *

Though their time in Canada had been exciting and joyous, Karma and Pemba were also ecstatic about returning to Nepal, and their village, where they would be able to see their family and friends again. Shortly after their school term began, we learned on a Skype call that Karma, with her new-found love of writing, had begun to contribute to the *Thrangu Express*, SMD's newspaper. She even began to encourage the younger kids to write stories, and published a reflection piece in the paper about her experience in Canada, which was a step forward for her, since she was not a girl who found it easy to share her feelings. We also heard the music and dance program Karma and Pemba and Chantal had thought up had been implemented at SMD – thanks to the girls' enthusiasm in bringing it forward (and also to Chantal, who presented it to Shirley and arranged the funding for it). When I asked Pemba if she had joined the dance program, she said she would, but only once she felt she had made enough progress with her studies. Having caught sight of the possibilities of a new world, Pemba was determined to realize them, and had set her sights on something much larger than what she had previously understood to be her future.

Her response reminded me of something she had said to me shortly before she returned to Nepal: "Mike, I'd like to have a conversation about my career and university path."

Taken by surprise, I had replied, "Pemba, it's great that you're thinking about this. However, you're only in fifth grade – you have lots of time to plan for this."

"Mike, I know I'm young, but my mind is old."

How the girls' lives will unfold, we do not know. But one thing is clear: during their year in Canada their minds had expanded greatly, in ways that would surely shape their futures, leading them on paths we might not even be able to imagine.

* * *

After our sunrise pause, Chantal and I set out again up the mountain, climbing in tandem, in the quiet solitude. Everything around us is still, and in the calm my mind is receptive, allowing moments with Karma and Pemba to keep surfacing. Moments, I know, that transcend time and space, and whatever changes will come our way. I think about what we've created together – a journey of souls – and I know it's the beginning of a much larger story, a story in which each of us will play our parts, but together we will forever be more than the sum of those parts.

ACKNOWLEDGEMENTS

First and foremost, I would like to thank my wife and partner in adventure, Chantal, for being wholeheartedly by my side on this great journey. I'd also like to thank my parents, and sister Marita, for all their support and love, and always looking out for me.

In helping to bring this book to fruition, I'd like to thank early readers and supporters Donald Loney, Sam Thiara, Chantelle Caron, Daniel Duane, Margo Talbot, Jan Redford and Sara Daly. A heartfelt thank you goes out to editor Beth Rashbaum, and to my agent Stephanie Tade for believing in me. I want to especially thank Don Gorman, and the entire team at Rocky Mountain Books, for bringing me into the RMB family.

An enormous thank you also goes to Arek Saczuk, Jason Kamin and Michael Averill for living their truths, passionately sharing their creative geniuses.

I'd like to thank everyone who made it possible for Karma and Pemba to visit Canada, in particular Dr. and Dr. Pasang Sherpa, Shirley Blair, Principal Acharya Wangchuk Tenzin and SMD Staff, as well as our family and friends and all those who made the girls' stay both welcoming and warm.

Last but certainly not least, I would like to thank Karma and Pemba and their whole family for their love and tremendous courage, and for accepting us into their family.

To learn more about the Shree Mangal Dvip (SMD) Boarding School for Himalayan Children in Nepal, please visit www.himalayanchildren.org.

NOTES

1 Wade Davis, *The Wayfinders: Why Ancient Wisdom Matters in the Modern World* (Toronto: House of Anansi Press, 2009), 3.

2 Steven Pressfield, *The War of Art* (New York: Grand Central Publishing, 2002), 146.

3 Luca Ventura, "Poorest Countries in the World 2019," Global Finance, April 17, 2019, https://www.gfmag.com/global-data/economic-data/the-poorest-countries-in-the-world.

4 "Nepal Country Profile," BBC News, February 19, 2018, https://www.bbc.com/news/world-south-asia-12511455.

5 "Buddha's Warriors," Al Jazeera, October 24, 2011, https://www.aljazeera.com/programmes/aljazeeracorrespondent/2011/10/20111017122121250153.html.

6 Anup Kaphle, "A Closer Look at the Dangerous Work That Everest's Sherpas Undertake for Western Climbers," *The Washington Post*, April 21, 2014, http://www.washingtonpost.com/news/worldviews/wp/2014/04/21/a-closer-look-at-the-dangerous-work-that-everests-sherpas-undertake-for-western-climbers/.

7 "Stairway to Heaven: How Deadly Are the World's Highest Mountains?" *The Economist*, May 29, 2013, https://www.economist.com/graphic-detail/2013/05/29/stairway-to-heaven.

8 Ibid.

9 Nareswor J. Gurung, "An Ethnographic Note on Nar-Phu Valley," Kailash – Journal of Himalayan Studies 5, no. 3 (1977), http://www.thlib.org/static/reprints/kailash/kailash_05_03_02.pdf.

10 His Holiness the Dalai Lama, introduction to *The Heart of the World: A Journey to Tibet's Lost Paradise*, by Ian Baker (New York: Penguin Books, 2004).

11 "Sky Burial," Travel China Guide, https://www.travelchinaguide.com/cityguides/tibet/sky-buria.htm.

12 "Namo Buddha: One of the Most Sacred Buddhist Sites in Nepal," Thrangu Tashi Yangtse Monastery, http://namobuddha.org/namo buddha.html.

13 Ibid.

14 Hannah Richardson, "Nepal Earthquake: 'Million Children Left out of School,'" BBC News, May 8, 2015, https://www.bbc.com/news/education-32624110.

15 Carole Cadwalladr, "Nepal Earthquake: The Village Wiped off the Map in a Few Terrifying Seconds," *The Guardian*, May 17, 2015, https://www.theguardian.com/world/2015/may/17/nepal-earthquake-langtang-village-everyone-was-dead.

16 Max Bearak, "Report on Nepal Protests Details Grisly Violence," *The New York Times*, October 16, 2015, https://www.nytimes.com/2015/10/17/world/asia/report-on-nepal-protests-details-grisly-violence.html.

17 Euan McKirdy, "Protesters in Western Nepal Kill Police with Spears, Axes," CNN, August 25, 2015, https://www.cnn.com/2015/08/25/asia/nepal-police-protester-deaths/index.html.

18 Saif Khalid, "India's 'Blockade' Snuffs out Nepal's Medical Lifeline," Al Jazeera, November 21, 2015, https://www.aljazeera.com/news/2015/11/india-blockade-snuffs-nepal-medical-lifeline-151121094929955.html.

19 Navin Singh Khadka, "Nepal's Forests under Threat over Fuel Crisis," BBC News, October 7, 2015, https://www.bbc.com/news/science-environment-34468821.

20 "Environmental Performance Index by City 2018," Environmental Performance Index, https://epi.envirocenter.yale.edu/epi-country-report/NPL.

21 Dennis Weinert and Patrick Weinert, "The Danger of Human

Trafficking Is No Secret in Nepal. Why Is It Still So Common?" World Politics Review, August 21, 2018, https://www.worldpoliticsreview .com/insights/25630/the-danger-of-human-trafficking-is-no-secret-in-nepal-why-is-it-still-so-common.

ABOUT THE AUTHOR

Michael Schauch is a mountaineer, entrepreneur and storyteller who lives to explore remote places around the world and to share the depth and beauty of human connection he discovers along the way.

With early success as an entrepreneur at age 15, and over 20 years of global financial investment experience, he brings his business acumen and altruistic heart to lead and support local and international mentorship, fundraising and educational initiatives. These include the education of girls and student mentorship in Nepal, outdoor youth leadership for those facing barriers to accessing nature, and holistic Indigenous leadership development in British Columbia. He holds an MBA from Queen's University and is a member of the Explorers Club.

He and his partner in adventure Chantal make their base camp in Squamish, nestled in BC's rugged Coast Mountains and temperate rainforests. Connect with Michael by visiting www.michaelschauch.com.